Jutta Portner
VIRTUAL NEGOTIATION

Jutta Portner

VIRTUAL NEGOTIATION

An Optimal Approach to Online Negotiations

Bibliographic information published by the Deutsche Nationalbibliothek
The Deutsche Nationalbibliothek lists this publication in the Deutsche Nationalbibliografie; detailed bibliographic data are available in the Internet at https://dnb.dnb.de.

ISBN (print): 978-3-96739-220-3
ISBN (epdf): 978-3-96740-447-0
ISBN (epub): 978-3-96740-448-7

Translation: Brandon Axley, Defiance, MO, USA
Editorial services by Anja Hilgarth, Herzogenaurach
Typesetting and layout: ZeroSoft, Timisoara
Cover design by Martin Zech Design, Bremen | www.martinzech.de
Photography © Lars Ternes, Zentralstudio e.U., Wien
Print on demand, Germany

Contents

A Word from the Author

Dear virtual negotiators, dear readers,

The pandemic has thrust us into the realm of digitalization, resulting in many of our everyday interactions no longer taking place face-to-face. Negotiations have not been immune to this, as they have been increasingly conducted virtually and continue to be today: conversations with your boss, your customer, even in private with your parents, within your circle of friends, with a craftsperson, or a service provider. Negotiations are a complex issue, with many parties involved and difficult topics, all of which are to be dealt with... from a computer? Let me reassure you: Such a situation presents both challenges and benefits. Many negotiators have already gained initial experience in this area in recent years. It works well most of the time, until it doesn't. What is the most important thing you need to achieve virtual negotiation success? Describe it in one word or with a brief phrase! In recent months, I have asked participants in my virtual negotiation training courses this same question. Here is what they said:

Active listening. Alternatives. Appreciation. Argument culture. Attention. Bandwidth. BATNA. Being muted. Beyond reason. Camera. Clarity. Clear goals. Coffee. Cohesion. Computer. Commitment. Confident leaders. Cooperation. Courage. Credibility. Culture. Culture of dispute. Depth. Dialogue. Direct contact. Directions. Discipline. Drive. Empathy. Exchange. Experience. Experimentation. Expressiveness. Eye-tracking software. Feedback. Fire. Flexibility. Focus. Fruitful results. Fun. Game. Getting past No. Getting to Yes. Gleam in the eyes. Hard work. Honesty. Inclusion. Information. Intensity. Interests. Joy. Laptop. Laughter. Leadership. Listening. Meeting links. Microphone. Motivation. Negotiation process. Objections. Objective criteria. Online platform. Opening. Openness. Passion for success. Peculiarities. Persistence. Praise. Questions.

Rapport. Reflection. Respect. Ring light. Rules. Sincerity. Sustainability. Sharepoint. Small talk. Softbox. Spirit. Strategies. Summarizing. Surprises. Teamwork. Team spirit. Tension. Thumbnails. Time. Togetherness. Trust. Understanding. Value. Will to change. Whiteboard. Will. WI-FI. Working together to achieve a goal. Zoom Fatigue.

If you want to know what exactly is behind all these exciting terms and how you can negotiate better virtually in your next workshop, family meeting, or client consultation, take a few hours of your spare time to read this book. That's all you need to do.

I wish you lots of enjoyment and insightful "aha!" moments.

Jutta Portner & the team at C-TO-BE. THE COACHING COMPANY

How this Book is Structured

This book consists of seven chapters divided into different practical tips. The first chapter, "Why Negotiating Online is Different than in the Offline World," highlights the differences between face-to-face and online negotiation and addresses concerns about this new and untested way of negotiating. The second chapter, "What Does Maslow's Hierarchy of Needs Have to Do with Online Negotiations?" employs this very model, which many of you are familiar with from motivational psychology, to understand what needs exist among virtual negotiators and how you can meet them. Chapter 3, "Well-Equipped from the Start," shows you how to successfully prepare for a virtual negotiation. "So Close and Yet So Far" is the title of the fourth chapter. Even in the online world, we cannot negotiate without contact and communication, and yet both function differently within the virtual space. Many of us know just how uncomfortable it is to speak into the void and not receive acknowledgement for our words or opinions. The fifth chapter, "Making the Most of It," gives you tips on how to overcome the limitations of body language. Even though we may be just inhabiting a little thumbnail on the other party's screen, we can still have a professional impact. In Chapter 6 "Yes, It's Possible! Exerting Influence in Virtual Negotiations," you will learn how best to proceed virtually, depending on whether you want to negotiate cooperatively or competitively. We also explore the challenges that can arise in remote negotiations and how you, as a negotiator, can best handle them. The final chapter, "Never Lose Sight of the Big Picture," demonstrates the importance of utilizing the first-mover advantage and leading right from the start. Only in this way will you retain control in your virtual negotiation. The terms remote, virtual, and online are used interchangeably in connection with negotiations.

The following stylistic devices will hopefully make the reading enjoyable:

VIRTUAL NEGOTIATION. TIP

In total, this book provides you with 25 tips on the most important topics related to virtual negotiation that have been comprehensively researched and prepared just for you.

VIRTUAL NEGOTIATION. KNOWLEDGE

You can never know too much. Take your time and find inspiration. Immerse yourself in uncharted territory. Here you will find some initial suggestions should you wish to delve further into individual topics. Every deep dive has a beginning.

VIRTUAL NEGOTIATION. QR

Looking for a YouTube video on how to choose the best microphone? Here's one that was tested for you by experienced professionals. Or what about a clip on the use of a concept board in virtual negotiations? A link to an expert has been selected for you. It is no coincidence that QR stands for "quick response." All you need to do is scan the QR code and you will be automatically redirected to quickly find all the information you need in a neatly organized format.

VIRTUAL NEGOTIATION. INTERVIEW

Behind C-TO-BE. THE COACHING COMPANY is a great team. Our experts share their knowledge on a variety of topics in short interviews. You can expect recommendations from a business actor, a yoga instructor, and two negotiation experts. We also interviewed an expert on the topic of deception in negotiations as well as an experienced virtual negotiator from a large German company.

VIRTUAL NEGOTIATION. THINKING TIME

Knowing the theory is all well and good. It is much more important to check whether the recommendations will also help you to succeed in the virtual space. Self-reflection is the key to change – and the big difference between experience and expertise. Only those who take the time to assess themselves will improve and become true virtual negotiation professionals. At the end of each chapter, you will have time to do so.

Short and sweet or in-depth? In this book, you can quickly find brief, clear-cut recommendations under the heading VIRTUAL NEGOTIATION. BEST PRACTICE. If you would like to delve deeper into the expertise, you will every now and then have the chance under VIRTUAL NEGOTIATION. READING MATERIAL.

VIRTUAL NEGOTIATION. BEST PRACTICE

"Best practices" are recommended practices, as well as methods for success or models of success that are used in the corporate world. They could also be termed recipes for success. Many strategies, tactics, and tools are equally effective when negotiating in person and online, yet there are always differences. This is exactly what you will find summarized under VIRTUAL NEGOTIATION. BEST PRACTICE, often following an initial discussion of general negotiation theory.

VIRTUAL NEGOTIATION. READING MATERIAL

For those eager to dive deeper, I offer valuable recommendations for additional reading that will help you uncover a greater understanding of the broader context. I provide insights that unearth your curiosity, motivating you to explore further. And from time to time, I share captivating gems that leave us all in surprising awe.

Online Negotiation: Is It Even Possible?

Negotiations have been taking place since the dawn of mankind. Ancient Germanic peoples undertook weeks-long marches to attend assemblies and make decisions on important matters. Marco Polo traveled along the Silk Road all the way to China in the 13th century to meet with business partners. And today, gamescom in Cologne is the largest trade fair for consumer electronics, where not only online games are presented, but licenses are also negotiated with partners from all over the world. Of course, this takes place in person, on location, and over coffee or a Kölsch beer – despite the astronomical hotel prices. For millennia, we have met face-to-face whenever it came to important negotiations. Couriers, letters, phone calls, and, more recently, emails or Skype calls have mostly been mere decorative touches to personal business meetings.

And then came the pandemic, when our world changed overnight. We were catapulted into the digital world, with all its yet uncharted rules and regulations. Today, it is impossible to imagine our everyday lives without online negotiations, which will continue to play a key role in the future even if we can and may meet again in person. Negotiating online, however, is a challenge for many people. Even brilliant negotiation professionals despair that their decades of experience in videoconferencing are not yielding the success they are used to. In online negotiation, things simply work differently, feel different, and no one really has much expertise yet.

Trust and dependability are indispensable elements of successful offline negotiation. To establish these prerequisites, negotiation partners meet over a cup of coffee, sit down at the negotiating table together, engage in discussions as equals, and seal their agreement with a handshake. Afterwards, the guests are invited to dinner together and toast to their success. None of this is possible with online negotiations. Instead of business lunches in fancy business attire and with sophisticated conversation, our personal lives are now inevitably spilling over into negotiations from our home office. Is your little son waving at the camera? Is your cat waltzing through the picture in search of affection? That's nothing to worry about at all. In fact, it's the opposite: It's something quite special, as a touch of real-life amidst all the professionalism makes us more human and fosters a sense of closeness. The kind of closeness that we can certainly use in holding negotiations based in trust. In the wake of the pandemic, communicating via screen in the corporate world has actually become a habit. We have now become quite good at holding team meetings virtually. Most negotiations today are also conducted via video call, but there is often still a lack of professionalism and levity. When there's a lot at stake, online negotiations present less obvious challenges as well as technical ones:

We are overextended: Negotiators are bombarded with numerous stimuli all at once. We are unfocused: Another incoming email here, another phone call there. We are constantly online and forget to take enough breaks. We are insecure: Who is reading along? Who is listening in? We talk very little or all at the same time. The virtual context makes communication and exerting influence more cumbersome.

Even for experienced negotiators, these kinds of negotiations are fraught with uncertainty. We have not yet cultivated sufficient expertise in remote negotiation. The Quadriga Hochschule in Berlin, in collaboration with the C4 Center for Negotiation, conducted a cross-industry survey of 185 companies in which negotiators were asked about their experiences in digital negotiation.

Here are a few select findings from the survey:

- For 75 percent of the surveyed companies, the proportion of digital negotiations before the pandemic was only 25 percent or less.
- During the pandemic, however, nearly 75 percent of respondents conducted 75 to 100 percent of all negotiations exclusively in a digital format.

- More than 70 percent consider digital negotiation to be significantly more challenging than face-to-face negotiation.
- Only 7 percent find digital negotiation less challenging.
- In about half of the companies, negotiation teams were trained and/or further qualified for face-to-face negotiations.
- Only 23 percent were trained and/or further qualified for digital negotiations.
- Almost 85 percent of respondents perceive the lack of personal contact as the greatest disadvantage of digital negotiation.
- For over 80 percent, the inability to read their counterpart's body language well is a limitation in digital negotiation.
- 61 percent find it very difficult to establish a level of trust in digital negotiations.
- More than a third see the multitude of misunderstandings as a major obstacle in digital negotiation.
- Overall, over 62 percent prefer face-to-face negotiation to any other form of negotiation. Only 20 percent of respondents prefer digital negotiations with online meeting systems. Telephone negotiation is the preferred form for just under 8 percent of participants.[1]

In "Virtual Negotiation. An Optimal Approach to Online Negotiations" you will learn how to overcome these challenges. It is well worth it, as online negotiation is here to stay. It's the new way of negotiating that is not only promising in its own unique way but also conserves resources: Travel times are reduced, and the time gained can be used more efficiently. Travel costs are avoided and the budget saved can be used elsewhere. Only those who familiarize themselves with the Best Practice tips will become virtual negotiation professionals.

Three reasons why it's worth reading this book and becoming an expert in virtual negotiation:

1. Virtual negotiation is new. Negotiators still have limited expertise and are insecure. Reduce your insecurities through knowledge and become a pioneer in this field.
2. Virtual negotiation has become a critical part of our everyday business practices. Invest in this skill and adopt a positive attitude.
3. Best Practice tips are clearly structured, developed by professionals for professionals, and easy for you to apply.

Before we dive deeper, let's first clarify a few basic terms: Is every conversation, every discussion, or every meeting automatically a negotiation?

What is a negotiation? A short definition

In the traditional sense, we talk about "negotiating" when individuals/parties have different interests and communicate with each other to reach an agreement.

This always requires four conditions:

- Mutual interdependence
- A conflict of interests
- An approximately equal balance of power
- Reaching an agreement is seen as the goal of the negotiation

Even though, of course, there can be conflicts of interest in private contexts and ideally a desire for agreement, in this book, I primarily focus on the professional context of a negotiation: when we are negotiating with service providers about the next order, tendering a pitch, or setting a price for our products and services. But negotiations also take place in business development with potential partners, or, as a leader, you might mediate a team conflict.

CHAPTER 1. Why Negotiating Online Is Different than in the Offline World

Many virtual negotiators report a great deal of exhaustion. Participating in several virtual meetings throughout the day means sitting at a desk for hours on end. In the evening, your back hurts, your neck and throat are tense, your eyes burn, and your head is empty. This phenomenon can be observed all over the world and even has a name: Zoom Fatigue. Of course, Zoom Fatigue also occurs in MS Teams, Google Meet, Webex, and Skype for Business. And the symptoms are always the same. Working remotely for long periods of time is tiring and stressful. However, there is a lot riding on the results that are achieved in business meetings. And of course, better results are achieved when virtual negotiators are not drained and depleted. Let's take a closer look at what exactly the stressors are and how virtual negotiators can deal with them professionally without falling victim to Zoom Fatigue.

We are exhausted: Too many stimuli, all at the same time

Who hasn't experienced total overload before? Too many windows are open, too many tasks popping up, too many things to do, and then your technology breaks down. One minute it was working and now suddenly nothing works. There's no use in clicking or restarting. The technology has gone on strike. By the time we finally get the problem under control, sometimes without knowing exactly how we did it, the meeting has long since begun. We stutter through an apology and are stressed even before we start negotiating.

The more negotiators participating in a session, the more thumbnails we see on our screen. Since the order of display is based on the sequence of log-ins, our own team's thumbnails are mixed with the other party's negotiating team. At first glance, it's not possible to make a clear distinction of the negotiating parties.

We don't even know where to turn our attention first: We've got the camera on, while the other person has their camera off. At the same time, we often work with multiple electronic devices. We're using a second monitor to simultaneously communicate with our colleagues via WhatsApp. Desperation can easily set in at that point. In order to maintain control and get off successfully despite a potentially bumpy start, we have to put a stop to excessive demands. But how?

It is important to first reassure yourself: A little stress won't hurt and is even normal. It pushes negotiators, making them feel activated, strong, and focused. Being challenged is helpful in moving a negotiation forward. But when we reach the breaking point, then disorientation takes the helm, and overwhelm (notice the last four letters of that word) becomes too much. We conduct an internal assessment of how much strength, energy, and attention we have. We compare this to the current demands. When we then subjectively feel that we're no longer up to the task and lack sufficient resources to cope, we become overwhelmed, and our body reacts. We become increasingly nervous, jittery, and simultaneously become aware of our behavior. This can contribute to a spiral of stress. The more stressed our body is, the worse we are at handling complex cognitive processes. Stress serves as an alarm function. The release of cortisol and adrenaline has always prepared us for fight or flight. However, running away or attacking doesn't help us at our desks, and thoughts like "I can't handle this" or "The negotiation is going to fail before it even begins" are not helpful. The more stressed negotiators are, the less focused they are, and the fewer creative problem-solving ideas they come up with. Therefore, it is an absolute necessity to get out of this stressed state as quickly as possible and act constructively rather than demeaning. So, what can online negotiators do?

Accept that it's just the way it is and quickly snap out of the stress pattern you find yourself in. Whether it's sudden heavy fatigue, a mental block, or frantic actions like clicking wildly, online negotiators must first remove themselves from the situation in which they feel trapped. Turn the camera off, take three deep breaths, glance out the window, take a sip of water – the key is to do something else briefly. And very briefly! Why? Because there's no time for anything longer when your negotiation partners are already online. But even small actions already give the brain a sense of self-efficacy, which we'll delve into in detail later.

We get distracted: Another incoming email here, another phone call there

People are naturally curious beings. It's only natural that we frequently tend to drift off. The surroundings of our negotiation partners are highly interesting. We try to decipher the titles in our colleague's well-stocked bookshelf. We wave to the cute daughter of a supplier and wonder about the boss's chubby cat that is walking through the frame. The visual stimuli in online negotiations are diverse. After every moment of distraction, our brain needs time and energy to refocus on the actual topic at hand and return to the original level of concentration. In self-management, this is referred to as the so-called "Saw Blade Effect." In addition, we have underlying thoughts: Negotiators often simultaneously think about the future and the past, about possibilities and impossibilities, about tomorrow and the day after tomorrow, and about yesterday and the day before yesterday.

To prevent a nervous breakdown, anchor yourself in the here and now. Here is a mindfulness training exercise that can be used quickly and anywhere: Say out loud, "I'M HERE NOW." While speaking, consciously focus on where you are at this moment and what you want to do now. Activate your senses and carry out a body scan, as it works wonders: Feel into your body, straighten up, and take deep breaths. Consciously smell something nearby, like an apple on the table or the coffee in front of you. "I'M HERE NOW" is a mantra. The more you repeat it, the more likely it is to become a routine that can effectively pull you out of the thought carousel and back into focused concentration.

We are constantly online: There's barely any time to catch our breath

What do you do when you're planning a long road trip? You start with a full tank, check the coolant, measure the tire pressure, and top up the windshield wiper fluid. You should approach video conferences in a similar way. It's important to be fully present and energized. Face-to-face meetings provide us with breaks as we move between meeting rooms, allowing us to catch our breath. Even brief moments of disengagement allow for small mental breaks that refresh us. However, online, in the worst case, one meeting follows the next. One begins right on the hour, while the next one starts at the top of the next hour, and this cycle continues for several hours. Sometimes, there's barely even a moment to grab another coffee or take a short restroom break between calls. How can we, in such a setting, bring certain topics to a conclusion, engage with new partners and their concerns, and make smart contributions in a focused way?

We get lost in the complexity and disengage

There's nothing to stop you from keeping several balls in the air. But keeping too many balls in the air is difficult for even the most experienced of jugglers. Trying to manage too many demanding topics during an online negotiation consumes a great deal of mental energy and often leads to us mentally disengaging much earlier than in face-to-face negotiations. Trying to manage too many mental tasks and operations simultaneously and in parallel is even more likely to fail online than in face-to-face negotiations. The myth that multitasking is a superpower still persists. But what should take priority among your many tasks?

outage. What needs to happen now? What is the minimum level of agreement you want to achieve before the lights go out? There are certainly tasks that you can recognize as being of lower priority and you can even delegate. It's best to take a piece of paper during your preparation and prioritize your topics into categories of HML (High/Medium/Low). What points can only and exclusively be negotiated by you? Which aspects do you not want to discuss in this online negotiation and will you postpone, and which might even be matters to which you can say no? Who can handle topics on your behalf? Take advantage of this opportunity. You are usually not the only person who can take on a task.

We are suspicious: Who is reading along? Who is listening in?

Instead of the three dimensions we have in face-to-face interactions, our perception of our conversation partners in online negotiations is reduced to just two dimensions. Intuitively interpreting body language, as we do in personal encounters, becomes much more challenging with "speaking-heads." We can only speculate about what's happening to the left and right, in front and behind the video thumbnail. If the background is blurred, we make guesses about where the other person is located: in a home office or on a workcation in another country? We may even wonder: Who's listening in today? Who might have access to confidential data? A healthy level of suspicion causes many negotiators to be more cautious with information. This, in turn, automatically leads to a slower development of trust.

Sometimes, there's no quick fix. When we feel overwhelmed in online negotiations because our assumptions about the other party are taking up a significant portion of our attention, it's often our inner beliefs that are to blame. In an online negotiation, we subjectively experience a high level of overwhelm. We feel stressed and entertain negative, stress-amplifying thoughts. However, there's actually a difference between *feeling* overwhelmed and *being* overwhelmed. We often contribute to our own sense of overwhelm. As negotiators, we believe we must achieve flawless results and be perfect. We must be liked by everyone, so we can't afford to disappoint, upset, or anger anyone. We must make anything possible. Often, we don't even question our beliefs anymore but carry them with us as if they were foundational truths. Like lighthouses, these beliefs guide us in our daily lives, showing us the direction we are heading, yet sometimes leading us in the wrong one. We tend to align ourselves with deeply rooted inner convictions, as if that's just how things are. However, there are times when it might be necessary to tackle the root causes rather than just treat the symptoms. Take a moment to question and examine your beliefs such as "Online negotiations are always difficult." Or: "Good business relationships can only be built through face-to-face negotiations." It's natural to be somewhat skeptical when negotiating online. Deep-seated convictions aren't easily shed. We often fall back into old patterns, especially when we are stressed. That's why it's crucial to stay vigilant and pause for reflection before, during, and after an online negotiation to make any necessary adjustments. A professional coach can also provide valuable support and empower online negotiators to initiate changes in their belief systems.

We prefer not to speak, or we all speak at the same time: The virtual context makes communication cumbersome

Who hasn't experienced a long moment of silence? No one says anything, or only rudimentary contributions are exchanged online. Some participants in an online meeting remain as silent as a post. It's uncomfortable. Extended pauses before someone eventually speaks require facilitators to endure the silence. Sometimes, they prefer to continue talking themselves.

The audio quality varies – sometimes for better, sometimes for worse. Sometimes this involves latency delays, crackling headsets, or negotiators hearing their own voice in the background as an echo from the other party. Communication in the virtual realm is often more challenging than in the offline world. Coordinating people's contributions is not easy either. In addition to the silence, there can also be a chaotic jumble of spoken remarks, with people chattering and rambling without pause. No one knows when the other party is finished, and multiple individuals speak simultaneously. This exhausting commotion can quickly fatigue the participants.

VIRTUAL NEGOTIATION. BEST PRACTICE

At the beginning of the call, actively address how you want to communicate during the online negotiation. Don't worry, it has nothing to do with selfishness but helps everyone involved as the discussion progresses. If something goes wrong during the conversation, consciously point out where and how the communication could be improved at that moment. Otherwise, nothing will change. Sometimes, people are overwhelmed because negotiation partners do not realize that they can no longer keep up. And why is that? It's because they keep nodding and smiling, not expressing what they really think, at most looking a bit desperate, hoping that the other party will interpret this expression correctly and realize what they need. But no one can read your mind or predict the future. So be sure to bring up any problems or concerns, and do it before it's too late. It's best to voice your thoughts when you're still in a constructive mood, rather than waiting until you're fed up, on the verge of exploding like a bomb, and on the brink of giving up. At that point, it's clearly too late. Address the manner of communication in a friendly yet resolute manner. Remember the 1st principle of the Harvard Concept: Be gentle with the individual and firm on the issue.

Many thanks to Lisa Kohlrusch from PACTUM for providing ideas on the challenges in online negotiations. In her blog post 13 Tips for Negotiating Successfully, the process consultant and mediator already offered valuable recommendations during the pandemic.[2]

VIRTUAL NEGOTIATION. THINKING TIME

In Chapter 1, we looked at how video-conferencing negotiations are different compared to face-to-face negotiations. Take a few minutes and assess your personal attitude on a scale of 1 for "not at all" to 10 for "completely" for an initial inventory of your mindset:

I feel exhausted: so many stimuli, all at the same time

Scale 1 10

I get distracted: Another incoming email here, another phone call there

Scale 1 10

I am constantly online and barely have enough time to come up for air

Scale 1 10

I get lost in complexity and disengage

Scale 1 10

I am suspicious: Who is reading along? Who is listening in?

Scale 1 10

We prefer not to speak or we all speak at the same time: The virtual context makes communication cumbersome

Scale 1 10

Analyze the six questions for yourself and draw a personal conclusion. Answers with a higher score call for further reflection and action. How can you change your attitude? What people, information, or tools do you need to make a change? Are there perhaps processes that need to be reconsidered and changed as well?

CHAPTER 2. What Does Maslow's Hierarchy of Needs Have to Do with Online Negotiations?

Many of us are familiar with Maslow's pyramid of needs under the popular term "Hierarchy of Needs." US psychologist Abraham Maslow gained worldwide fame for his simplified depiction of human needs and their significance for motivation. His theory found its way into many other sciences. It is dealt with in economics, organizational psychology, and also in philosophy.

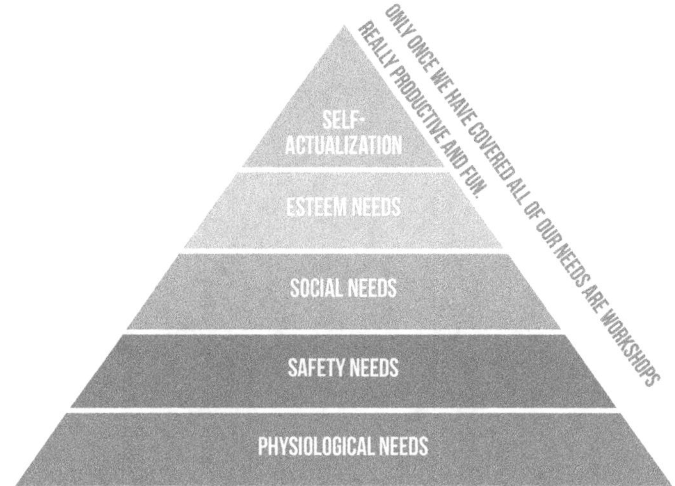

The idea behind the Hierarchy of Needs is based on the assumption that there are different types of needs that influence our satisfaction and, consequently, our behavior through various elements and effects. Maslow observed that some needs take precedence over others. Maslow does not consider it helpful to draw up specific rankings.

However, needs can be roughly categorized into five major areas for general guidance. He starts with the basic ones, the physiological needs and the safety needs. These are followed by social (love needs) and individual needs (esteem needs) up to the highly developed human need for self-actualization. Based on this, Maslow explains that needs can either be satisfied or unsatisfied. Unsatisfied needs are called deficiency needs. As long as a need remains unsatisfied, it influences and triggers our actions in a way that we seek to fulfill it. With increasing satisfaction of a need, the urge to act to satisfy that need gradually diminishes. When our stomach is no longer growling, we no longer constantly think about food.

Let's take a closer look at the significance of the five levels of needs in the context of virtual negotiation. We will first examine what each level of need generally entails, then assess what is different in virtual negotiations, and in the third step, we will give you recommendations and you will learn about tools that can make online negotiations more productive. First, let's look at physiological needs:

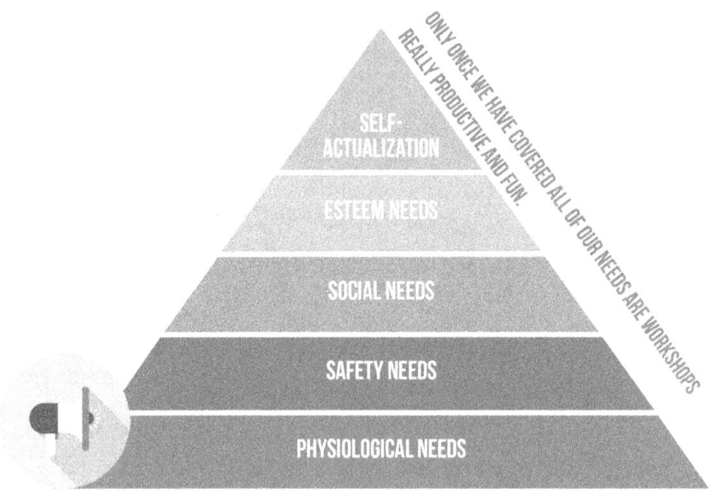

Physiological needs: To hear well. To see well ... and much more

Physiological needs are basic needs. They are necessary for the preservation of human life. Does the room in which we sit have a pleasant indoor climate? Negotiators don't want to freeze or sweat. Hunger and thirst also need to be satisfied. A healthy breakfast and sufficient water at the workplace contribute significantly to being able to work in a concentrated manner. We need enough oxygen to breathe. Stale air decreases attentiveness, and well-ventilated rooms counteract this. The posture of our body also plays a big role in negotiating in front of the screen. Do I have an office chair that I can sit on comfortably for a long period of time? Is my posture straight, or does my back hurt? When negotiating virtually, can I clearly hear what is being said, or is there crackling and rustling in the background? Can I clearly see what is being presented, or have the thumbnails with the faces of the negotiating parties been shrunk to the size of postage stamps? Moreover, it's extremely frustrating for negotiators that such a significant portion of their attention is eaten up by trying to cut through the clutter and decipher text on densely packed slides. Last but not least, the perception of the environment also plays a major role: Is someone's 15-year-old son playing a computer game in the background and fighting with his gamer gang? Is someone's neighbor next door getting their roof replaced accompanied by the constant sound of roof tiles being thrown into the dumpster? Is the colleague at the desk opposite you on the phone with her rather penetrating voice? It is not difficult to understand how great the influence of satisfied physiological needs is on one's well-being. From the filled coffee pot to the opening of the window before the negotiation to the review of the presentation technology – up to now, these things have been the responsibility of the host. Now, it's up to each and every virtual negotiator themselves.

Physiological needs in the digital space. What's different?

Negotiators are no longer in the same room together. Everyone is sitting alone at work or in a home office. This means that each virtual negotiator is responsible for the provision of food and drinks as well as for a pleasant room atmosphere and a healthy working environment. The quality of what can be seen and heard also depends to a large extent on the technical solutions chosen. In addition, virtual negotiations do not encourage physical activity, meaning that the negotiator also assumes this responsibility as well.

VIRTUAL NEGOTIATION. BEST PRACTICE

Before starting an online negotiation, familiarize yourself with the technology, test out any tools, and make yourself a cup of coffee or tea. Here's another quick tip: Create a pre-negotiation checklist that includes all of your physiological needs in one place and check them off, item by item, as you prepare!

Physiological needs in the digital space: Tools and methods

We require four channels for a good collaboration in the digital space:
- Visualization tool, for example, a digital whiteboard for digital post-its
- Sharing service or a cloud solution to make content available to others
- Video conferencing tool, ideally with a gallery view of the negotiators to enable real-time communication
- Communication tool with email and chat function; this also enables real-time communication

Virtual negotiators must be able to see two things equally well: each other and what's being negotiated. Therefore, use two screens if possible.

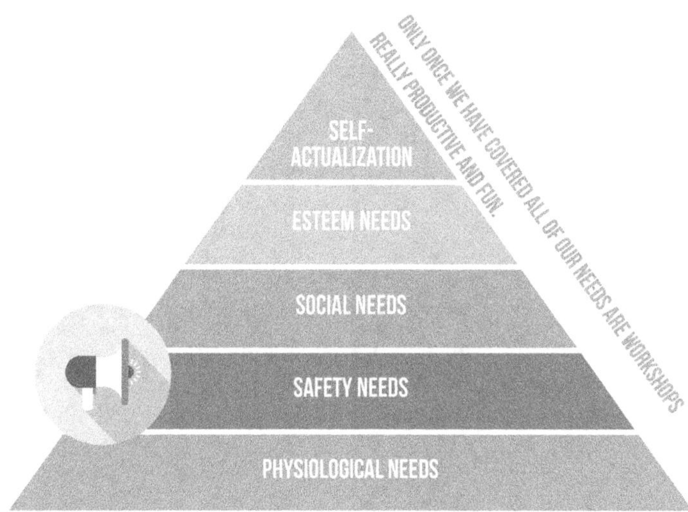

Safety needs: So much to discuss. So much technology ... HELP!

Once physiological needs are mostly satisfied, safety needs begin to emerge. When people feel safe, they feel they are in control. They are relaxed. A lack of security, on the other hand, means tension and a feeling of uncertainty due to a lack of control. This leads to stress and a sense of acute danger. According to Maslow, in a broader sense, the search for security and stability is also reflected in the human preference for the known over the unknown. Furthermore, humans strive to explain unknown phenomena and to understand connections. Finding a protective person who can be trusted to take charge and lead the way also provides us with a sense of security.

Physiological needs in the digital space: What is different?

Digital technology, tools, and working methods are new to many people and sometimes associated with reservations. That's why good preparation is crucial to the success of virtual negotiations – for both sides. It's helpful to provide participants in advance not only with the agenda, but also with tutorials and assignments. Because only when everyone feels comfortable with the situation and with the technology will a necessary sense of security emerge to enable constructive negotiation.

The role of those conducting negotiations also serves as a lever to skillfully convey a sense of security. The calmer and more relaxed the facilitators, the more relaxed the participating negotiators. Because technology must be mastered as an additional element in an online negotiation, attention spans are also shorter in virtual negotiations.

Physiological needs in the digital space: Tools and methods

All negotiators should feel comfortable in the digital workshop space. The hurdles are often new tools and methods, not so much the motivation. Warm-ups and short explanations help to get to know and understand the interaction in the often-unfamiliar environment. Especially those negotiating virtually who have been working with specific platforms for a while sometimes forget that the same familiarity with technology might not always be the case for colleagues on their own team or partners from the other party. It is important to create a trusting environment and encourage participants to ask questions about the technology and talk about their uncertainties at any time.

To eliminate any kind of obstacles, all participants should already know exactly which technique and tools will be used before the negotiation and have a basic understanding of them. Information and preliminary exercises can be provided in the digital whiteboard or file hosting service to provide training on the use of the tools used in the virtual negotiation. The negotiators' level of digital training is therefore key to the set-up and execution of a virtual negotiation.

VIRTUAL NEGOTIATION. BEST PRACTICE

When negotiating online, more preparation time is needed for everyone and everything.

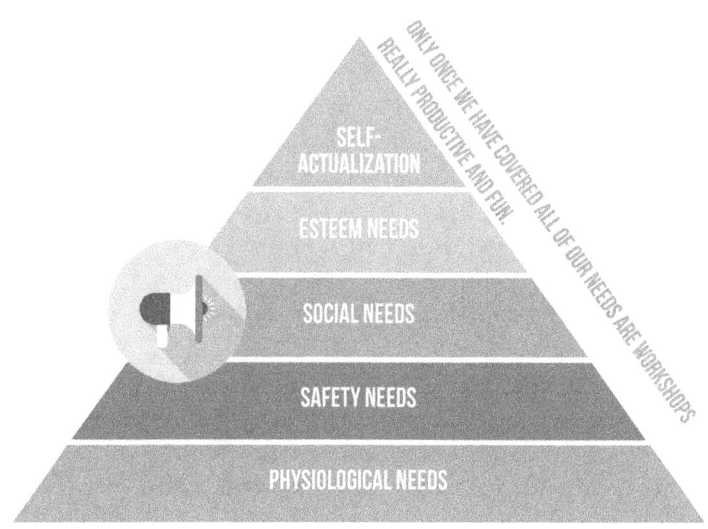

Safety needs: So much to discuss. So much technology ... HELP!   **35**

Social needs: Team spirit? Online? More lone wolves than ever

Once physiological needs and the need for security are satisfied, we experience an increased desire to establish social relationships. Connectedness manifests itself in many different ways: in personal friendships with colleagues, sometimes even with suppliers or customers, in team spirit, or in a sense of belonging to people with similar interests. As social beings, we strive for interaction with others, community, and mutual support. Positive relationships foster fondness and collaboration. The absence of connectedness can be an extremely demotivating factor. People then invest energy to close this gap. If they are not successful, frustration, inner resignation, or the breakdown of relationships will result.

In addition, we take on certain roles in groups. In a dynamic balance, relationship systems are constantly changing. The need for attention always brings together the giving and receiving of attention. That's why we constantly try to influence the perception of others, so as not to come across as ignorant, disruptive, or incompetent, or even worse: to feel diminished, embarrassed, or become an outsider.

A digital gathering is not the same as sitting in a room together. In this context, it's important that we make good use of the available channels and consciously create space for the kind of social interaction that usually takes place unconsciously.

Social needs in the digital space: What is different?

The negotiation atmosphere is largely created through a shared presence in one location. Online negotiators can compensate for this lack of togetherness through some appropriate methods and the awareness that the situation is "different." Conducting virtual negotiations is purely a matter of practice. The more experience negotiators have, the easier it becomes to maintain the relational aspect.

In the digital realm, there are always two spatial dimensions: the one from which we are following the virtual negotiation (e.g., the office or workspace) and the digital space where the negotiation is taking place. This means that all negotiators connect from separate spaces into the shared digital one, creating the same starting point for everyone. Work is performed in this abstract space where participating negotiators are coming together. Groups are generally not ready to work from the beginning; they need time to "get acquainted." What is the current mood? How are the negotiating parties doing? How does my role compare to the others? Where do I stand? Of course, these questions are not discussed openly, instead, online negotiators work them out quietly within themselves. There are many lone wolves in the virtual world, and consequently, they can also be found in online negotiations. At the same time, employees repeatedly state that they have lost touch with the team when working from their home office. They feel "disconnected." Online negotiators also want to belong to a team, form a community, and experience mutual support. It is just important to give it time.

Social needs in the digital space: Tools and methods

From small talk to big talk. Even if it's uncomfortable, don't jump right into the topic at hand. Treat each other with respect and appreciation, allow each other to get settled in first. Emojis and reactions (e.g., thumbs up, clapping hands) can be used deliberately to convey emotion. This is particularly suitable for the overture (warm-up) and the conclusion (feedback) of the online negotiation.

When leaders of an online negotiation recognize the significance of social needs, they will pay special attention to them and consistently integrate them into the negotiation process. "Contact before contract" is a powerful motto that online negotiators can use to guide them.

Focus on silent participants and those who are still struggling with technology and tools! It is easier to lose sight of them in a digital setting.

Work with the camera turned on as often as possible. This, too, is a valuable investment in building a relationship between the virtual negotiators.

Talk to your negotiating parties not only about your thoughts, but also about your mood. Utilize tactical empathy.

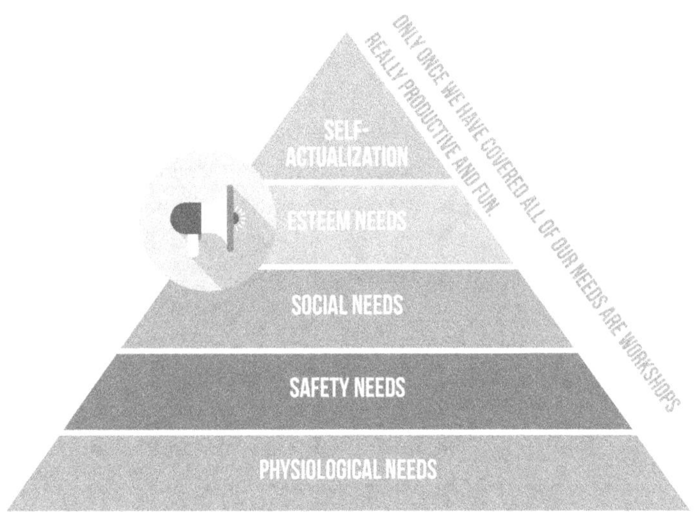

Esteem needs: Notice me … please!

Esteem needs refer to the needs of the individual, such as the desire for mental and physical strength, success, as well as independence and freedom, and the aspiration for recognition, prestige, appreciation, respect, and significance. Seen in this way, an esteem need is a passive component of self-esteem that can only be fulfilled by other people for us. People want to be noticed. Even in the virtual world.

Esteem needs in the digital space: What's different?

What do online negotiators wish for in remote negotiations from others in order to get their esteem needs met? They want to be understood both rationally and emotionally. To demonstrate rational understanding, it is necessary to listen attentively, ask questions, and paraphrase. It's not always easy in the virtual space, but it is certainly possible. Empathetic listening is the appropriate tool to show emotional understanding. This is more challenging from a distance. Empathy is easier to achieve when negotiators can see the other person and perceive and mirror their nonverbal reactions. Online negotiators also wish to be able to voice their opinions and perspectives and for their negotiation partners to be able to understand their viewpoints. This confirms to negotiators that they are on the right path and builds self-confidence.

The role of a facilitating person is highly recommended in a remote setting. In addition to know-how in the steering of the negotiation, classic facilitation skills are particularly important online. Closely linked to this is the appropriate selection of communication methods.

Esteem needs in the digital space: Tools and methods

Remember: Speech is worth its weight in gold! Explanations of the process often need to be more detailed in the digital realm so that all virtual negotiators can follow along. Questioning looks, a furrowed eyebrow, or an uncertain mood are more difficult to perceive non-verbally in the digital realm because it is not possible to make contact remotely with the person sending such signals without being noticed. Here, it's also important to remember: Ask questions. Follow-up. Review. Adapt. Negotiators' experience in digital working also plays a major role here and ought to be the deciding factor in the selection of methods, just like in an offline setting. Explain things as clearly and unambiguously as possible. Repeat explanations until everyone knows what to do. For a skillful division of tasks, take a co-facilitator with you into the online negotiation. Individual assistance or the short-term solution of technical problems are handled by the co-facilitator so that the main facilitator can stay on track. Create small task packages with short time slots and clearly defined tasks. Encourage remote negotiators to actively address suggestions and requests regarding virtual negotiation. A little practice and courage may be needed here. Facilitating also means directing and steering in the digital space. An additional focus is on the available channels. Periodically ask for interim feedback from negotiators. Regularly summarize interim results as well, emphasizing what you have already accomplished.

Self-actualization: Activate and encourage a desire to create

Self-actualization is a trendy term that is used time and again by everyone from esoteric yoga teachers to dynamic start-up founders.

But what does Maslow mean by self-actualization? Maslow formulated the following characteristics that he attributed to self-actualizing individuals: a significantly greater sense of composure, even curiosity in the sense of joyfully embracing stimulating challenges of the unknown and uncertainty. Also, a strong acceptance of one's own weaknesses and shortcomings as the result of an uninfluenceable natural reality. Furthermore, Maslow attributed self-actualization to spontaneity, simplicity, and naturalness. In connection with self-actualization, however, Maslow no longer spoke of motivation, but of unfolding. Self-actualizers, according to Maslow, possess a great deal of free will, a keen eye for objectivity, and a high degree of autonomy. They feel sympathy and affection towards fellow human beings, which Maslow referred to as the "older brother" attitude. People want to find meaning and fulfillment, including in their work. It's always about intangible values as well. Negotiators want to actively shape outcomes, not waste time on unnecessary matters. Their actions should make sense and achieve a clear higher outcome, with negotiators consciously leveraging their strengths in the process.

Self-actualization in the digital space: What's different?

While experienced negotiators with the capacity for self-actualization can intuitively assess situations and needs well in the offline setting, the digital setting requires even more attention from them. Methods that work well offline are not automatically suitable for the digital space. It can happen that self-actualizing individuals overwhelm their negotiation partners and, in the process, lose them. They are driven to focus on the overall purpose of the negotiation. In doing so, they may overlook the "lesser" needs of remote negotiation partners, especially in the assumption that everything is okay because it is for them. Shorter, more focused virtual negotiations are often more practical to ensure everyone can keep up.

Self-actualization in the digital space: Tools and methods

How can the need for self-actualization be accommodated in online negotiations? Assess the meaningfulness of the goal to be achieved and present it explicitly. Re-think certain methods. Let creative minds work together in small groups. Agile methods or even creativity techniques are ideal. The characteristics of an online negotiation even offer advantages: Multiple small sessions with tasks for "in-between" can often be integrated into the negotiation more effectively than the traditional full-day negotiation. Take advantage of online setting options, such as working in break-out rooms, and collaboration software like Miro or Conceptboard.

VIRTUAL NEGOTIATION. THINKING TIME

In Chapter 2, you learned why satisfying needs is important for negotiators to feel comfortable and achieve good results in negotiations. You now know the five levels of Maslow's Hierarchy of Needs and their significance for virtual negotiations. Before your next negotiation, take a few minutes to consider which of the needs have already been met and which needs you still want to fulfil:

- Physiological needs: To hear well. To see well ... and much more

- Safety needs: So much content. So much technology ... HELP!

- Social needs: Team spirit? Online? More lone wolves than ever

- Esteem needs: Notice me ... please!

- Self-actualization: Activate and encourage a desire to create

....

....

....

....

CHAPTER 3. Well-Equipped from the Start – Successful Preparation for Online Negotiations

Let's first take a look at when you can negotiate online and in which cases you should definitely conduct face-to-face negotiations. In the next step, you will understand why it is helpful to know the negotiation process well, down to the smallest detail. By doing so, you will prevent negotiations from going around in circles. This is already something that is quite burdensome in face-to-face negotiations. In online negotiations, it can be a deal-breaker for participants if negotiation partners walk out in frustration because arguments are being exchanged for the third time in a row or the negotiation has hit a dead end. Furthermore, good preparation involves the adept handling of your technology. This allows you to focus your attention completely on the participants and the topics at hand. You will learn why it is advisable to limit the number of participants and sessions to ensure a smooth flow. Last but not least, we identify security risks and explore ways to minimize them to the greatest extent possible.

Decide first! Auction or negotiation? Virtual or in person?

In purchasing, auctions are considered an easy and fast way to achieve the best result. This opinion is widely held. Most consumers are familiar with platforms like eBay, where items as diverse as umbrellas and garden lawnmowers are auctioned off. A fierce bidding war ignites for a used luxury handbag, while Grandma's coffee set gathers dust in the digital world as well. It seems like there's nothing that isn't being auctioned off. It is already a common practice for commodity buyers to conduct e-auctions with suppliers. E-auctions are also a type of online negotiation. In their book *The Art of M&A*, a reference book on handling mergers and acquisitions, authors Stanley Foster Reed and Alexandra Reed Lajoux write: "Auctions are still considered the best strategy to get the best price."[3] This common belief likely contributes to the fact that even entire business units or subsidiaries are auctioned off. And since the selling price is determined through competition among bidders, no executive has to fear facing criticism for it. Among the best-known auction theorists are Professor Jeremy I. Bulow from the Stanford Institute of Economics and Professor Paul Klemperer from the University of Oxford. Together, they have developed a theoretical model about auctions and bargaining that confirms the conventional wisdom about the value maximization effect. They concluded that "due to the independence and risk neutrality of bidders, an auction with n+1 bidders is preferable to a negotiation with n+1 bidders." The result suggests, according to Bulow and Klemperer, that the additional competitive component is of greater value and advantage than well-developed negotiation skills.[4] This is contradicted by Guhan Subramanian, a professor at Harvard Law School and a renowned negotiation expert, in his book *Negotiauctions*. "Every auction comes with significant disadvantages and risks that neither theoretical models nor common wisdom draw attention to."[5] Subramanian points out the ongoing debate about the appropriateness of online auctions in procurement. Auctions and bidding processes (tenders) have significantly reduced operational procurement costs. Software providers such as Aruba Networks and SAP, which make e-procurement child's play, have played a major role in this. The awarding of contracts to suppliers is simply handled via online tenders. Suppliers' offers arrive in real-time, and almost simultaneously, the procurement team can select the most cost-effective offer, thus generating substantial savings for the company. In the late 1990s, a veritable flood of e-auctions swept the procurement industry. However, the initial overwhelming enthusiasm waned as companies often had to learn the hard way that crucial non-price decision criteria cannot be represented in an e-auction. Even if prices can be compared easily, it is difficult to see whether the cheapest offer is also the best in terms of quality. As a result, buyers started to differentiate between commodities (standardized and therefore comparable goods) and demanding goods and complex services. The latter were procured through traditional negotiations. However, the suppliers also learned from this. Fewer and fewer participated in e-auctions. One reason was that less profit could be earned due to the price competition. In addition, the market underwent consolidation, and neither the suppliers who weren't awarded contracts nor those who were very price-competitive had any interest in establishing strategic partnerships with customers when it came to jointly solving problems.

- **Definition of auction**. An auction is a special form of price determination. Characteristic of the auction process is that the seller becomes a merely passive participant once the auction process has begun. Competitive pressure arises from competing bids from bidders. There are several variations of auctions:
  - ▶ **Open auction:** One characteristic of an open auction is a transparent process, meaning that bids are made vocally or by raising one's hand, making the current highest bid known to all participants. Various types of open auctions include:

▷ **English auction:** Low initial bid, 50 percent of the expected minimum bid; bid increments are initially large and decrease as the auction progresses.

▷ **Reverse auction:** Here, initially there is a high starting price, which is then gradually reduced. Buyers and sellers switch roles. This means buyers are process designers, and sellers are bidders.

▷ **Dutch auction:** The Dutch auction is characterized by a high initial price that is gradually lowered by the auctioneer. Due to their speed, Dutch auctions are suitable for time-critical decisions.

▷ **Japanese auction:** In a Japanese auction, the initial price is low and is gradually increased. It also features high speed and is therefore also suitable for time-critical decisions.

▶ **Sealed-bid auction:** One characteristic of a sealed-bid auction is that the process is not transparent. Bids are submitted in writing by bidders and kept hidden. Other bidders do not know the value of each other's bids. Bidders often don't even know the number of other participants, so a competitive situation can be simulated even in the absence of competition. There is often an indicative (non-binding) preliminary round (longlist), followed by an invitation from the buyers to a second round with 4 to 8 interested bidders (shortlist). After a thorough due diligence examination, a final and best offer is requested. There are also various types of sealed-bid auctions:

▷ **First-price sealed-bid auction (blind auction):** A first-price sealed-bid auction is characterized by a process in which all bidders simultaneously submit their bids – formerly in sealed envelopes, today all at once – online. No bidder knows the bids of the co-bidders. The bidder with the highest offer wins and pays the price they offered.

▷ **Sealed-bid second-price auction (Vickrey auction):** In the sealed-bid second-price auction, bidders also submit their maximum bid. The bidder with the highest bid wins the auction but only has to pay the price of the second-highest bidder.

> ▷ **Request for quote:** An RFQ is a request for a quotation to selected suppliers for a specific product or service. An RFQ can be requested either alone or in tandem with an RFP (Request for Proposal – which provides more detailed information about the product). An RFQ is requested when the standard product and its price are already known, there is an existing business relationship with the supplier, and the process is ongoing.

■ **Definition of negotiation.** A negotiation can also involve a price determination or the resolution of a conflict of interest that extends far beyond that. The dynamic interaction between both parties is a characteristic of the negotiation process.

The right decision: e-auction or negotiation?

Making the right decision is not always easy. E-auction or negotiation? What are the advantages of an e-auction and what are the advantages of a negotiation? Assuming your company has the necessary software and processes in place to conduct an auction, here are some key arguments in favor of auctions: Auctions are usually quicker to conclude than face-to-face negotiations. There is no personal contact between the buyers and bidders, no off-topic conversations, no small talk, and no resource-consuming socializing. No heated emotions, annoyed glances, or sharp comments. No phony friendliness or long-winded explanations. Buyers become passive participants in the auction, which many see as an advantage for the reasons previously mentioned. Furthermore, auctions provide the highest possible transparency, and prices can be compared by the buyer in the best possible way. If the asset can be specified precisely, then many potential bidders can be approached without the need for costly and time-consuming negotiations with individual partners. Time is gained that can be used elsewhere. Competing bids and offers increase competitive pressure. In addition, reinforced by the prevailing opinion that auctions always yield the best price, participants alleviate internal justification pressure within their organization.

However, there are also several reasons that favor negotiation: If personal relationships and the manner in which business is conducted are important because a long-standing partnership exists and the intention is to continue pursuing a close strategic business partnership, there is no way around a negotiation. Respect, appreciation, and acknowledgement can only be expressed through direct contact. If there are large differences between the best offers, then it is necessary to find out what the reason is, and this also only works through dialogue. Another reason could be that the bidders have a strong BATNA (Best Alternative To a Negotiated Agreement) meaning they have attractive alternatives to work together with other partners. In this situation, it is the responsibility of the buyers to persuade others to collaborate with them. In general, the dynamic interaction between the participants plays a major role. Are you looking to explore new opportunities and think outside the box together? This only works in a negotiation, not in an auction. What if the supplier is a monopolist? An auction will not lead to the desired success in this situation. A situation in which the relationship between business partners is accompanied by joint investments in innovation, research, and development also speaks for offline negotiations, especially when qualified experts can contribute their expertise. Expertise is no substitute for software. In this context, we are talking about a low risk tolerance. This means that there is little willingness on the part of customers to take a risk associated with the decision to use new suppliers. Business developments that involve confidentiality are typically conducted exclusively in personal negotiations.

The following is a brief overview that can be used as a decision-making tool.

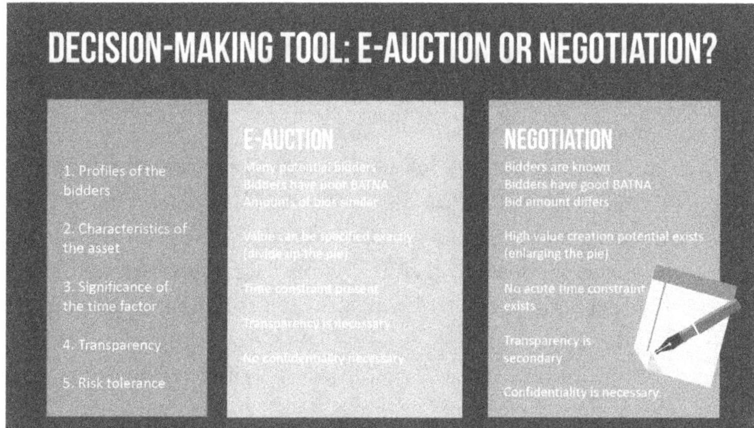

Now, after considering all the arguments against an auction and in favor of negotiation, the question remains: in person or online? Before you send out your invitations, carefully consider what you want to achieve and which format is more suitable for it.

There are situations where there is no way around a face-to-face negotiation. Whenever possible within the selected negotiation situations, opt for a face-to-face meeting. Unless the next lockdown prevents a face-to-face meeting or one of the parties is quarantined. Here are the cases in which I recommend a face-to-face negotiation:

- **Face-to-face negotiation for kick-off events:** The first meeting is a worthwhile investment in the negotiators' future relationship. Further negotiations can then be carried out online.
- **Face-to-face negotiation for joint problem solving:** If difficulties have arisen that could jeopardize further cooperation, it is imperative to attend in person to get to the bottom of the problems and solve them. By doing so, you show how seriously you take the situation and the priority you attach to it by making the effort to make a personal appearance.
- **Face-to-face negotiations for conflict discussions:** Conflict discussions are held between employees and supervisors when

emotions have already boiled up and de-escalation is urgently needed. It is important to negotiate in private, ideally in a quiet place. The ability to perceive and correctly interpret nonverbal reactions plays an important role.

- **Face-to-face negotiations for special cases requiring mediation:** If parties are so at odds that they are unable to resolve their conflict on their own, a mediator can work wonders by mediating between the parties and facilitating an agreement. In mediation and conflict resolution, the perception of the mood, represented by body language, also plays a crucial role. Conflict resolution is understood to be a dispute resolution method as an alternative to governmental court proceedings. With the help of a third party, solutions are found outside of a court room.
- **Face-to-face negotiations to forge alliances:** If you are looking for partners with whom you want to form coalitions, be it blocking coalitions or winning coalitions, then this works best in an in-person negotiation. One major advantage here: confidentiality. You know who is listening, as well as who is not!
- **Face-to-face negotiations for salary negotiations with employees:** Salary negotiations are stressful for many employees, especially and precisely because they are not conducted very frequently. In this case as well, it is more appropriate to meet in person and discuss matters calmly.

VIRTUAL NEGOTIATION. BEST PRACTICE

Online negotiations are suitable for all other situations than those mentioned above! Make yourself aware of the many benefits.

- **Online negotiations with part-time participants:** A major advantage of online negotiations is that experts can be invited at specific times to share their opinion or expertise with the other negotiators. This prevents negotiators from wasting their time without contributing anything useful to the negotiation.

- **Online negotiations with participants from different locations:** It has now become widely known that significant costs are saved when travel expenses and travel time are eliminated. Instead, other tasks can be performed, and we are also doing something good for the environment. Another sometimes underestimated factor is also our nerves, which we spare by not being stuck in traffic, not squeezing through crowded security checks at airports, not chasing lost luggage at the Lost & Found, not waiting for delayed trains on drafty platforms, and not spending nights in uninspiring business hotels.

- **Online negotiations when participants are very busy:** There are some employees whose schedule is fully booked. It's difficult to schedule a meeting with them; they've hardly got any availability for months. A slot for a one-hour online negotiation on a specific topic is easier to find than a half or full day.

- **Online negotiations to minimize status differences:** Virtual negotiations make status differences less obvious. The thumbnail images all have the same format. No one is larger than the other. For now, everyone has the same space available to them, from the personal assistant to board members.

- **Online negotiations to clarify issues spontaneously:** An online negotiation can be arranged quickly. This makes you much more flexible to deal with issues. Online negotiations are definitely a format that is very conducive to mental flexibility. Got a brilliant idea? Just invite a few colleagues, the client joins in, and a new option is explored.

- **Online negotiations to have access to files at any time:** This is arguably one of the greatest advantages of virtual negotiations: to have unrestricted access to all the necessary data stored on our servers. Have you received a spontaneous question from the other party? No problem! The necessary answers can be provided with just a few clicks. No longer do we need to print anything, which also conserves resources and saves costs. No printer paper, no printer cartridges, and less waste after the negotiation.

- **Online negotiations to be able to perform research at any time:** Do you have a new customer and want to have a look at their reference list during the negotiation? Want to take a look at the management organization chart? Or check out the candidate's background on LinkedIn? In online negotiations we have access to the Internet, and any information we desire is available to us in a matter of seconds. What a luxury!

- **Online negotiations for quick consultation with colleagues:** Want to quickly create a break-out room and switch to mute to discuss the next move with your colleagues? This is easy to do in virtual negotiations. At the same time, it offers the huge advantage of working as a team and aligning your own perceptions with those of the negotiation partners during the meeting.

- **Online negotiations to make it easier to say no:** Being able to say no is important in negotiations. And it's easier online than in face-to-face negotiations. We all surely remember the icy atmosphere after failed in-person negotiations. As soon as a firm "No" or "That's not up for negotiation" is thrown into the mix, things often get pretty frosty. In the virtual space, we can recover conversations more quickly and end or adjourn them if necessary. And a "That's a bit difficult right now!" is still the verbal alternative we keep up our sleeve to avoid slamming the virtual door shut completely.

- **Online negotiations to take more frequent breaks:** Breaks are important to stay energized and reenergize. During breaks we satisfy our physiological needs, giving us time to take a moment to relax, step out onto the balcony, or go for a walk around the block in order to clear our minds for the next mental feat. After breaks, small disagreements can dissipate, with the virtual negotiators coming back with renewed energy.

DR. MIRIAM STEIMER

Dr. Miriam Steimer is the Senior Director in the Strategy Mergers and Acquisitions division at SIEMENS HEALTHINEERS and has extensive experience in virtual negotiations.

J.P. Virtual negotiation is efficient: Negotiators can concentrate fully on the matter at hand, with no travel time, no lunches, and no dinners together either. Not even shared coffee breaks. Is this a blessing or a curse?

M.S. During "coffee" or "breaktime" chats, I've received many interesting insights in in-person negotiations and sometimes information that would not be openly discussed in a large group. Unfortunately, this aspect is entirely absent in virtual negotiations. What remains is speculation or simply missing knowledge, which can sometimes delay the development of possible strategies.

J.P. What kind of positive experience have you had with virtual negotiations so far?

M.S. Through thorough preparation and asking many questions during the meeting, successful outcomes can be achieved even in virtual negotiations. Intensive preparation, in my opinion, involves the drafting of a coordinated meeting agenda with all parties, which allows each side to prepare accordingly. Pre-reads are also essential, especially for complex topics, to ensure that negotiation partners are on the same page. I recommend the facilitator to allocate the right amount of time for each topic, including organizing breaks. It's better to plan a little more time for each topic and for breaks, so that each side has enough time for internal coordination.

M.S. Then it's better to take a break instead of continuing. Also, it's important to remember that there are no stupid questions. Create an environment in which anything can be asked. Facial expressions and gesturing are limited, and feedback is somewhat restricted for the negotiating party. This makes it harder to respond and react to the negotiators. That's why negotiations should never be held without a camera!

J.P. Technical challenges and a poor Internet connection always result in disruptions. Even today, not all participants are familiar with Teams, Zoom, etc. What can be done?

M.S. One "basic" recommendation to follow is to ensure in advance that all participants are familiar with the technology, at least within your own team. Also, define: Who will speak first? How will coordination take place? Who will take notes? And who will step in if the technology breaks down? For face-to-face meetings, you should keep your laptop closed unless it's absolutely necessary. I also recommend closing any emails and/or other programs that could distract you during a virtual meeting. This will stabilize the connection and help maintain full focus on the negotiation.

VIRTUAL NEGOTIATION. TIP #2

The new way to prepare for a negotiation: Close to the negotiation process

Every negotiation undergoes a distinct process. If you are aware of the individual phases, you have a predefined agenda to guide you. Consistently following the thread of a negotiation provides you with the opportunity to steer the conversation. You won't overlook any of the steps that logically build on each other and make sense from a psychological point of view. A virtual negotiation consists of seven phases[6]:

- Preparation
- Overture
- Gaining clarity
- Developing solutions
- Making a decision
- Conclusion
- Follow-up

THE NEGOTIATION PROCESS

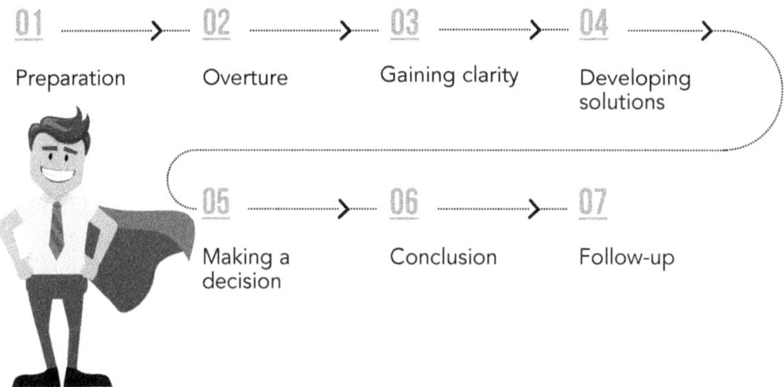

In each of the individual phases, it's important to consider specific productive aspects in order to achieve a sustainable outcome in the end. The negotiation process is independent of the negotiation style, you can follow the same steps to negotiate either cooperatively or competitively. Let's take a closer look at each of the individual phases in detail.

NEGOTIATION PROCESS

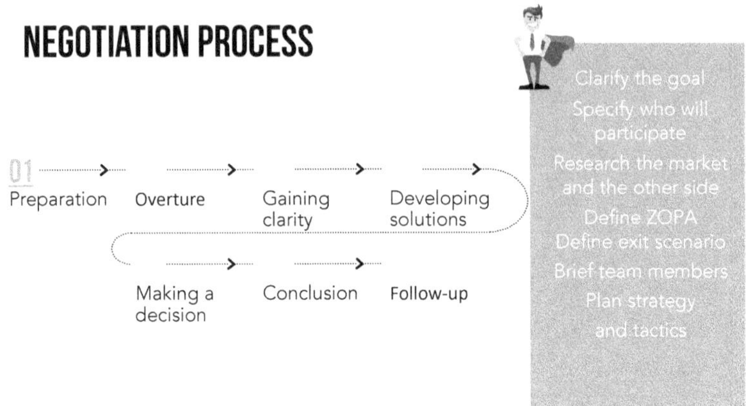

The preparation

In the *preparation* phase, you set the direction: What is it that you want to achieve? First and foremost, you need to get clarity about the higher goal. From this, the focus on emphasizing cooperation or competition in the upcoming negotiation arises. Subsequently, this will depend on the planning of your negotiation style, tactics, and arguments. What kinds of scenarios are you likely to encounter? Clarity about this will help you prepare your specific goal, as well as your argumentation, strategy, and tactics. You identify your negotiation participants and know who from the other party will be participating in the negotiation. You gather background information about the other party and are familiar with the negotiation history. You establish your exit scenario (reservation point) and define your ZOPA (Zone of Possible Agreement). If you are negotiating as a team, be sure to schedule enough time in advance for your team members to agree and commit to the joint strategy. The amount of time you spend on preparation depends on the following factors: How complex is the topic? How important is the result to you? What is the value of the negotiated asset? Is this the first time you've met the other party, or can you clearly gauge their approach? How extensive is the necessary research? Is this a one-time negotiation, or are you aiming for a longer collaboration? What is your personal negotiation experience? Are you an old hand and able to improvise? Or do you have little experience, and precise preparation would provide the necessary confidence to react flexibly? The adequacy and amount of preparation can, therefore, vary significantly. One rule of thumb is that preparation takes about as long as the negotiation itself. Being well-prepared gives you a stable foundation, providing support and boosting your self-confidence. It also allows you to occasionally refer to your materials during the negotiation to follow the process closely.

VIRTUAL NEGOTIATION. BEST PRACTICE

The early bird catches the worm. Start your preparation early. Use a one-pager, which is ideally a single-page document with a limited number of subcategories, ensuring you don't get distracted while searching for bullet points. Send all required documents to all parties for review BEFORE the negotiation. Keep the one-pager handy as a guide during the negotiation and make additional notes during the negotiation about new information from the other party. Good preparation is a sign of respect and a first-rate investment in the relationship with negotiation partners.

NEGOTIATION PROCESS

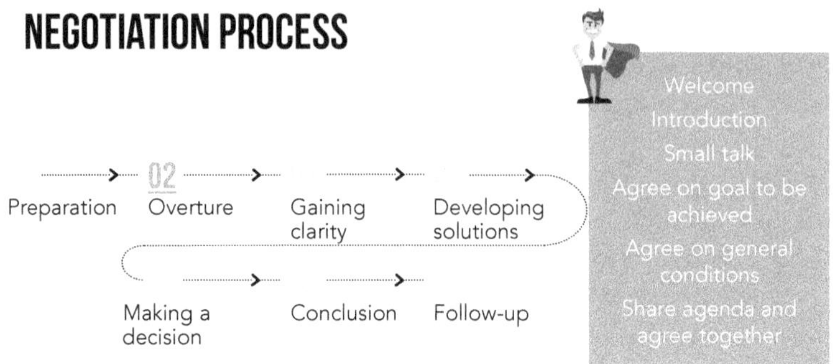

The overture

The *overture* is a term used in music. It sets the tone and establishes the mood. In the first moments you can hear whether the piece is in major or minor, whether it is a cheerful operetta or a tragic opera, a melancholic, powerful Bach oratorio, or a banal pop song. When we come together with other people, we are not able to work immediately and at the push of a button. First, we try to get a sense of the atmosphere. What will the atmosphere be like when we arrive? Does the other person like us? Is there an air of reserved professionalism, or is there an underlying sense of animosity? We take time to connect with each other and have a keen sense of who is taking control of the negotiation. In secret, even the first few minutes are about a demonstration of negotiating power. For this reason, negotiators first discuss harmless topics in the overture. Both sides try and "size each other up." In face-to-face negotiations, the greeting sets the tone. Here we can already observe who is shaking hands with whom and how. Is the other person's hand coming from above, signaling dominance right from the start? This is not possible in virtual negotiations. Here, we pay more attention to whether the greeting is brief and matter-of-fact. If it is, the online negotiation is also likely to be concise and to the point. Or are the parties taking time to build trust through small talk, disclosing some initial, perhaps even private, things about themselves? Is the other party receptive and open, interested right from the start? In this case, a spirit of openness can develop that allows trust to grow. In face-to-face negotiations, the negotiation atmosphere is also determined by the choice of venue and the seating arrangement. This is neither possible in virtual negotiations. We can't offer drinks here. Many years of observation have time and time again confirmed that the start predicts the finish! Another element of the overture is to introduce the negotiating parties and their roles at the outset, and to communicate the objective and agenda. Why are we here today, and what do we want to have achieved by the end of the negotiation? Organizational matters and the time frame are also discussed. Do we have an hour or the entire day available to us? Will there be any follow-up appointments that necessitate finishing on time, or is there some flexibility at the end, should we be in the flow of things? Many negotiators underestimate the significance of the overture, even in face-to-face negotiations. As the negotiation progresses, they may realize that there might be different interpretations of the objectives. They may not be aware of who is playing what role in the opposing negotiation team, or there may simply be no agenda to help get the negotiation back on track when conversations start going in circles. In virtual negotiations, the overture is even more important.

VIRTUAL NEGOTIATION. BEST PRACTICE

Make use of the first-mover advantage and take control of the conversation right from the beginning. Ask whether all parties to the negotiation agree to you taking over the facilitation. Address your negotiating parties by their names. As often as you can! And with the right one. To do this, prepare a sheet of paper with the names and various roles, especially of new negotiators. This gives you the ability to quickly see who is in which role. Think in advance about possible topics for small talk and allocate time for the *overture*.

NEGOTIATION PROCESS

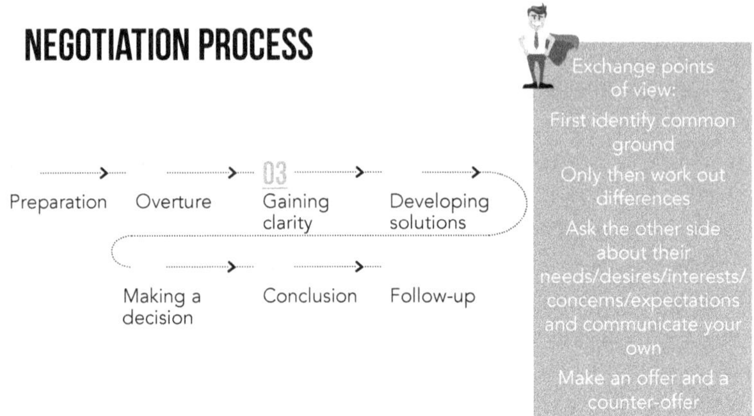

Gaining clarity

Gaining clarity means not fishing in murky waters. According to the definition, one of the criteria of a negotiation is the existence of a conflict of interest that needs to be resolved. Therefore, this phase is often referred to as the *exploration phase*. The goal is to explore, to investigate where the common ground and differences between the negotiating parties exist. An already prepared needs and requirements analysis will assist you in this phase to gain a better understanding of the true motives and reasoning of the opposing side. You can clear the fog of ignorance especially with the help of questions. Since there are always at least two parties in a negotiation, there will also be at least two different sets of interests. Don't forget to make your own interests known and to explore the interests of the other party. In negotiations where you are interested in cooperation, it can happen that you are too focused on trying to understand with a positive attitude and, in the process, forget to express your own standpoint clearly and precisely. Perhaps out of fear that this would adversely affect the atmosphere. In competitive negotiations, you will likely disclose very little and aim to learn as much as possible about the other party. The motives of the other party are of little interest to you in competitive negotiation.

When negotiating, there is always common ground as well. The smallest common denominator is often the intention to reach an outcome; otherwise, the negotiation wouldn't be taking place. Experienced negotiators understand that it is good to agree as often as possible to get as many "yeses" as possible: "Agree wherever you can" is their recommendation. The first "yes" is an important step on the long journey to the final "yes," which is the approval of the negotiation outcome. The final stage of the exploration phase is the disclosure of the positions. Demands are made, facilitating the transition to the *developing solutions* phase. If thorough work is not done in the gaining clarity phase, negotiators will soon find themselves going in circles and returning to the previous phase. Hasty solutions will not be satisfactory because important motives have not been taken into account. Therefore, at the end of the third phase, be sure to summarize what you've understood and obtain agreement to proceed to the next step. Negotiation experts see this phase as the key to negotiation success.

VIRTUAL NEGOTIATION. BEST PRACTICE

Especially in virtual negotiations, this phase is often not given enough time. Negotiators increasingly stick to their assumptions without examining them. Questions seem more laborious than in face-to-face negotiations. But just ask them anyway. Ask. Ask. Ask plenty of open-ended questions. Ask follow-up questions; that is, use the responses of the negotiating parties to build on and ask the next question. Ask even more questions than in face-to-face negotiations! Summarize the other party's answers and confirm what you have understood. Avoid asking questions one after the other, because, especially in virtual negotiations, only the last question heard is likely to be answered. Allow the other party time to come up with answers and to formulate them. Online, it is often much more uncomfortable to endure pauses and silence. Bite your tongue whenever you feel the urge to interrupt the other party and respond prematurely. In virtual negotiations, allow the other party to summarize what they have understood from time to time. Keep a conversation going by repeating the last three to four words you heard. This encourages the other party to keep talking.

NEGOTIATION PROCESS

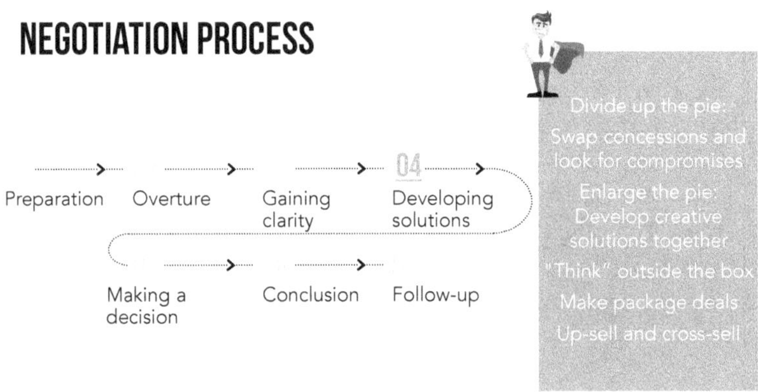

Developing solutions

This phase is the heart of the negotiation. The parties involved in the negotiation develop possible concrete approaches to resolve the conflict of interest. The general conditions have been clarified and initial demands have been made. Negotiators bring into play the options that offer them the greatest possible benefit. Concessions are exchanged. This is where the rules of concession kick in:

1. Use the anchoring effect when it comes to making the first offer.
2. Immediately doubt the adequacy of the counterbid.
3. Impress the other party through your apparent price transparency.
4. Dance the dance of negotiation and continue to get closer through small steps.
5. Go through at least three rounds of negotiation.

6. Make a final, non-price-related demand just before closing the deal.[7]

In cooperative negotiations, the goal is to seek a consensus that satisfies both parties. Sometimes the negotiating parties even manage to enlarge the pie and find creative new ways to find solutions. Ideally, packages are put together, creating added value that negotiators couldn't have imagined beforehand. In so-called distributive negotiations, on the other hand, a type of competitive negotiation, the pie must be divided. Both sides try to get the largest possible piece of the pie. Negotiation tricks are used to their own advantage. Often there are winners and losers, or the parties compromise. In distributive negotiation, however, a compromise is always only the second-best option, because neither side can enforce its maximum demand in the process.

VIRTUAL NEGOTIATION. BEST PRACTICE

While distributive negotiation works surprisingly well in an online setting, cooperative negotiation tends to suffer. Why is that? Cooperative negotiation requires a trusting relationship, a mutual understanding of interests, and time to jointly develop creative solutions. Just like in brainstorming, negotiators inspire each other by contributing their own ideas, picking up on others' ideas, and further developing them. If you want to explore whether the pie can be enlarged, you need to know the methods. Two important rules of brainstorming: 1. Come up with as many ideas as possible, and in virtual negotiations, it's advisable to document these in writing. Ideally, this is done on a shared document, because otherwise valuable insights can be lost too quickly. 2. Separate the evaluation from the collection of ideas. To ensure that virtual negotiators adhere to this rule, it is advisable to address it even before coming up with the various options: "Are you willing to first gather some possible solutions and then evaluate them afterward?"

NEGOTIATION PROCESS

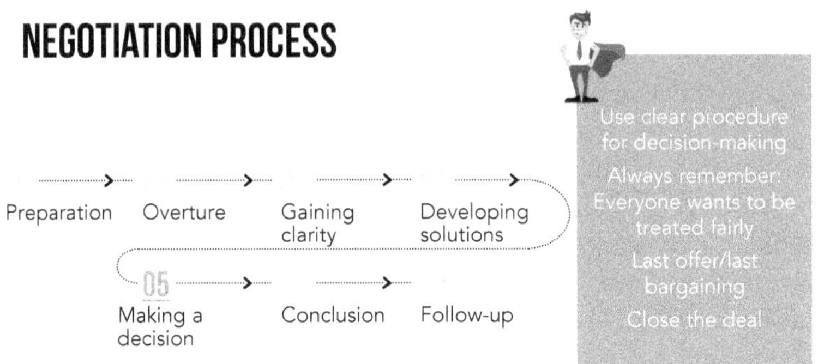

Making a decision

The negotiation is nearing a conclusion. To ensure fairness, participants in cooperative negotiations will agree on criteria that are independent of individual interests and will ensure a fair, transparent procedure. The goal is to make the decision-making process transparent so that it can be followed and understood by all negotiators. Bringing transparency into the decision-making process is the primary objective here. In competitive negotiations, objections are typically addressed in this phase, and closing techniques are employed before reaching a deal. The last offer, for example, is a clear signal that the negotiation is nearing its conclusion. During this phase, delay tactics or time pressure can be observed as tricks to gain a unilateral advantage. Professional negotiators will now engage in an internal dialogue and compare the potential outcome with their reservation point, which is the minimum they want to achieve, and their BATNA, which is their plan B. If the potential outcome is better than your alternative outside the negotiation table, you will decide in favor, otherwise against it. In face-to-face negotiations, the handshake is traditionally used to seal the agreement.

VIRTUAL NEGOTIATION. BEST PRACTICE

When engaging in cooperative negotiation, consider in the preparation phase which methods and objective criteria can help you arrive at a clear outcome. Slow down if your negotiating party is still hesitant and pause the virtual negotiation. The ability to quickly put negotiations on hold and take a short break in order to coordinate is a distinct advantage of virtual negotiation. In face-to-face negotiations, extra rooms need to be booked, or negotiators have to travel to the site again, which involves a much greater effort than opening a break-out room or quickly coordinating over the phone. It's important that you can communicate with your own team privately using an alternative communication channel. Don't use the chat from the main meeting for this purpose, as it can be read by all participants. Always present interruptions as an advantage for both sides and make use of this opportunity as often as you like. Remember: "Go slow to go fast." Demand breaks if the other party is exerting pressure.

NEGOTIATION PROCESS

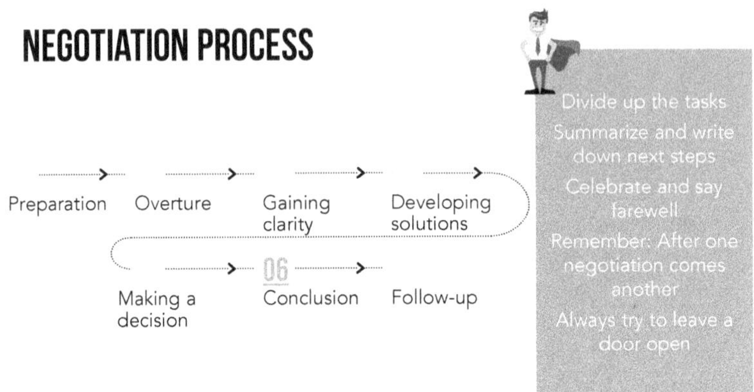

The conclusion

The *conclusion* of a negotiation is divided into two steps: the content part and the formal part. For the content part, the parties summarize the results once again. They discuss how to address any remaining issues and plan specific next steps. In the formal part of the conclusion, if the parties are satisfied, they will congratulate each other on the negotiation outcome. The negotiation often concludes by revisiting topics from the beginning of the negotiation, allowing participants to transition from big talk to small talk. The farewell officially concludes the negotiation. In many face-to-face business negotiations, the negotiators often go for a meal together afterward, extending the official conclusion beyond the actual negotiation. This is also where the foundations for future business encounters are laid because one negotiation is followed by another.

VIRTUAL NEGOTIATION. BEST PRACTICE

In virtual negotiations, the "soft" part of the conclusion is often left out. The decision is sealed with a nod, the next steps are discussed, and a brief goodbye is waved into the camera, provided it is switched on. Very often, there is no more small talk, and instead of a shared meal, participants find themselves alone in their home offices or at the office in front of their computers. While introverted individuals may sometimes be relieved not to have to engage in further socializing, extroverted negotiators can sometimes be left with a sense of emptiness. For both parties, a few kind words about how the negotiation went and confidence in the implementation of the outcome are a valuable investment in future collaboration. Because online, too, the saying holds true: After one virtual negotiation comes the next. Just as we part ways, we also come back together.

NEGOTIATION PROCESS

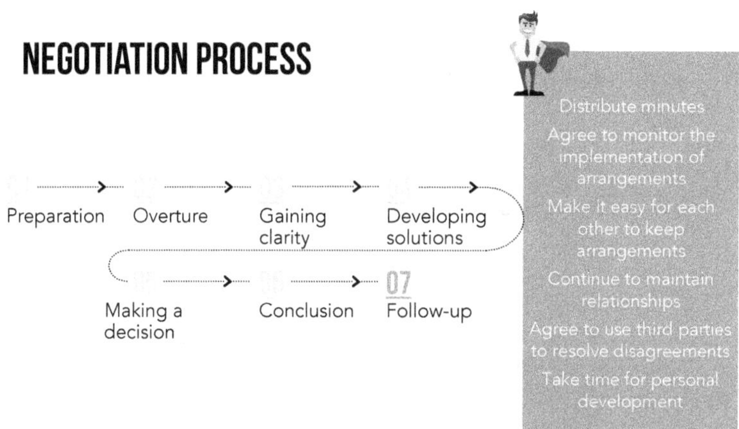

The follow-up

One of the most typical elements of post-negotiation is documentation: The results and also the further implementation of the next steps agreed upon in the negotiation are recorded in the minutes or contract. To be able to pursue to-dos effectively, the ICN model (Informed/Consulted/Negotiated) has proven to be useful: Negotiators make a distinction regarding who is merely informed about the outcome (Informed), with whom negotiators are to consult further to discuss the subsequent strategic direction (Consulted), and who the future points of contact are for further negotiations (Negotiated). However, individual *follow-up* is a phase that often gets overlooked in many cases once the collective follow-up is completed. If the negotiation is successful, negotiators tend to stop thinking about it, and often, it's their everyday business routine, with all its tasks and demands, that compels negotiators to immediately dive back into their daily work. This is unfortunate, as personal reflection provides a rare and valuable opportunity to assess and expand one's negotiation skills. If negotiators have engaged as a team, they can provide each other with feedback. What worked well for us? What kind of things can we rely on? What will we do differently next time? Where can we improve? The lessons learned can be documented in writing. This allows you to take a quick look at the notes before the next negotiation and gradually become more and more professional.

VIRTUAL NEGOTIATION. BEST PRACTICE

The minutes of an online negotiation can often be more easily created if a file was collaboratively worked on during the negotiation. All participants have insight into the content and are aware of the current state of affairs. In contrast to face-to-face negotiations, where the minutes are written afterward, this approach can save time. A second option is to create minutes of the proceedings or a simultaneous record. Those leading a virtual negotiation can also delegate this task. Agree not only on the outcome but also on the implementation of actions in day-to-day business. Also, specify who will oversee the implementation and what steps are to be taken in the event of difficulties. For example, a neutral person or institution can be designated as an arbitrator.

Short on time? Use a one-pager for quick preparation

In keeping with the negotiation process, it has proven effective to establish the seven phases of negotiation as a foundation during the preparation phase. One advantage of this is that it increases the likelihood of not going round in circles during the actual negotiation and not jumping back and forth in the process. When negotiators lose track and begin to only react to the actions of the other party, it leads to a loss of control, creating a dangerous dynamic. The negotiators give up control and risk surrendering control over the negotiation to the other party. Negotiators run the risk of becoming more susceptible to influence and manipulation. Most negotiators are aware of the significance of comprehensive preparation for negotiation success. Nevertheless, good preparation often doesn't take place. Why is that? Mainly because of the time we don't take.

VIRTUAL NEGOTIATION. BEST PRACTICE

With a one-pager, you need no more than a single sheet of paper to prepare yourself briefly, concisely, and precisely.

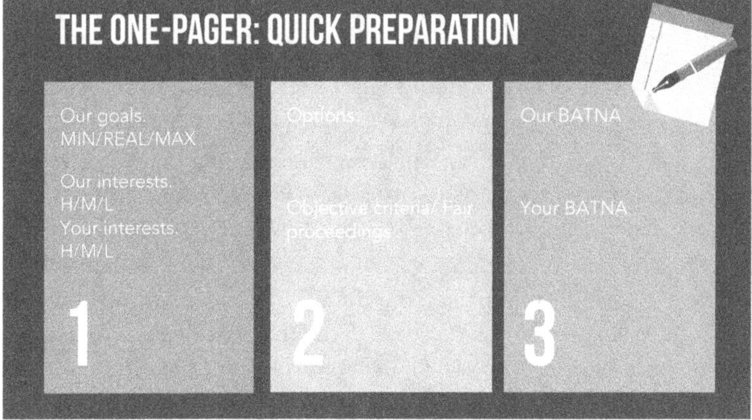

Less is more: Limit the number of participants

In a survey on what the optimal number of participants in a negotiation should be, the answers would likely vary widely. Some of you might say, "two people," and justify your response by explaining that with only one counterpart, the most in-depth exchange is possible. In such a reduced setting, you can listen best, have to process the least amount of stimuli and information, and it costs the least energy, likely getting you to your goal more quickly. "But," a few other negotiators might interject, "in a team, we can achieve much more." Strengths are distributed more evenly, both factual and subtle information can be reliably absorbed, we can exchange behind-the-scenes information with our sparring partners, and as a team, we are less susceptible to misjudgments and incorrect strategic decisions.

So, when is it worth negotiating alone, and when is it better to negotiate as a team? What is the maximum number of negotiators in virtual meetings?

From main speakers, support speakers, and observers: How to professionally utilize roles in your own team

There are certain negotiation situations where you must decide whether you want to negotiate alone or as part of a team. You weigh the advantages and disadvantages of showing up without support and being entirely self-reliant. Alternatively, the situation may force you to appear as a team. Especially in a professional setting, hierarchies play a crucial role, and decision-makers must be present in negotiations, just like the specialists in certain areas who can assist the negotiators with advice and assistance. What are the characteristics of each role? Knowing these will make it easier for you in the future to decide whether to go into your next negotiation alone or with helpful support.

When is it worth negotiating as a team?

- When it comes to highly complex topics and issues, because many eyes and ears see and hear more.
- When expertise is required from various experts, because "Nobody is perfect!"
- When both specialized and cross-disciplinary interests need representation, as these may well differ in certain aspects.
- When you want to get the best out of all four areas – communicating, listening, keeping the minutes, and facilitating – because a single person can quickly reach their limit.
- When you want to show strength, because you present yourself as a collective force and not as a lone fighter.
- When you need moral support, because together you feel stronger.
- When you need to protect certain individuals, because they are serving as witnesses.
- When you don't trust one another, so that you can hear what is said and agreed upon.
- When you need to admit mistakes or fault, so that you can distribute the burden among several shoulders.

When is it worth negotiating alone?

- When it concerns minor matters and involving everyone would be too cumbersome.
- When you want to save costs, because the more people participate in the negotiation, the more expensive it becomes for you.
- When it concerns straightforward topics in which you don't require experts.
- When you want the other party to think it's a minor issue.
- When you need to resolve a dispute privately, because it's easier without witnesses.
- When the other party trusts only you personally, because confidentiality can be better maintained.

- When there is an obligation of confidentiality, because the smaller the circle of those in the know, the easier it is to keep things secret.

VIRTUAL NEGOTIATION. BEST PRACTICE

If you negotiate alone, especially in online negotiations, it can be useful if you have limited decision-making power. This way, you can always negotiate time for post-corrections and avoid being pressured into making hasty decisions without reflection and consultation. Even if you do have decision-making authority, you can set a strategic barrier by saying: "I need to first clarify this with my supervisor/the department head/the board/my partner..."

The recipe for success: Fewer people who communicate better

Negotiation is communication. The four fundamental pillars of communication are:

- Speaking articulately to express one's own interests.
- Active listening to understand the interests and demands of the other party.
- Taking notes to visualize and record what has been said.
- Actively steering the negotiation to not lose sight of the intermediate steps and the goal.

Further subtleties, such as individual strategies and tactics, are then built upon this foundation. Without a stable foundation, success in online negotiations is also on shaky ground.

An experienced negotiator may be able to handle all four tasks simultaneously in face-to-face negotiations. However, true professionals, especially in virtual negotiations, seek support and delegate as many tasks as possible to have more capacity for higher-level, strategic drivers.

Imagine you want to build a house. How do you proceed? You begin with architectural planning, from calculating the structural stability to digging the excavation pit. Then comes the structural work, followed by the interior finishing. Electrical wiring needs to be routed, heating needs to be integrated, and plumbing work must be completed. Then comes the tiling and painting. Very few will handle everything from start to finish entirely on their own. Most of us on experts, and in most cases, an experienced construction contractor coordinates the various building phases. The contractor thinks ahead, never losing sight of the big picture – a finished house. They hold the reins and steer the construction project toward the desired goal. Participants in a negotiation have precisely this expectation of the facilitators. In very many cases, the roles of facilitator and lead negotiator merge. Often this is due to practical reasons, as it's more cost-effective when a host can also take on time management and the keeping of the minutes.

What are the four roles that can be actively assumed in virtual negotiations?

- The role of the facilitator
- The role of the main speaker
- The role of the support speaker
- The role of the observer/recorder

Let's clarify the four roles. What exactly are the associated tasks before and during a virtual negotiation? At the end, you can consider which of these roles you will take on in your future online negotiations to fully leverage your team's potential.

The role of the facilitator: Looking out for others by knowing how to steer a negotiation

What would happen if no one felt responsible for steering the negotiation? Side conversations? Arguments? Endless repetition? Premature results? Loud negotiators would probably prevail much more often than reserved participants. Virtual negotiations especially need facilitators in order to keep the negotiation moving, otherwise there is a risk that it will get bogged down or side-tracked. The online facilitator gets negotiators talking to each other on an equal footing, as, otherwise, only the dominant individuals would speak, and the shy ones wouldn't get a chance to. Building an atmosphere of trust is also one of the facilitator's tasks, as this does not usually happen on its own. Likewise, the facilitator mitigates conflicts, which requires steering know-how. Last but not least, the facilitator ensures that the virtual negotiation leads to a clear agreement and that participants do not leave without results. Who should provide the facilitator? You or the other party? The rule is: Take control, maintain control, and don't relinquish control to the other party! But feel free to relinquish the facilitation and share the control if desired. What are facilitators' tasks before the negotiation? Facilitators invite participants and send the proper link. They send the agenda with the objective, purpose, and duration of the negotiation. What are facilitators' tasks during the negotiation? Facilitators are responsible for introducing participants. They introduce the negotiation leadership, employ suitable methods, and utilize collaborative media. The sequence of speaking is coordinated, and the negotiators are addressed by name. The agenda serves as a guide to keep the negotiation on track and allows for topics to be removed if a deadlock is imminent. In addition, a facilitator regularly summarizes results in between and at the end.

The role of the main speakers: Providing leadership in virtual worlds, too

Most of the time, it's the main speakers who have the largest share of speaking time during a negotiation. But what are main speakers' tasks before the negotiation? They discuss the negotiation topics with the team, prepare the negotiation both strategically and tactically, plan the initial demands and concessions, and draw up a list of questions. What are main speakers' tasks during the negotiation? They come up with a shared and flexible agenda, but contrary to what their name might suggest, they don't speak too much, but mainly listen. They could also be called main listeners. When main speakers do speak, they are articulate, precise, and concise in their language. They are responsible for finding common ground and developing alternatives, with "What if...?" being a proven guiding question. They object when necessary and follow the rules of concession when it comes to resolving conflicts of interest.

The role of the support speakers: Through the eyes of the specialists

Support speakers are experts who assist the main speaker. With those true specialists by their side, main speakers can remain at ease, knowing they don't have to know everything. What are support speakers' tasks before the negotiation? They prepare their own topics and align them with those of the team, in addition to being briefed on the collective strategy, tactics, and agenda. They also work with all other participants to develop a list of questions, demands, and concessions. Preparation is conducted in virtual pre-meetings. What are support speakers' tasks during the negotiation? When it comes to their own topics, they wait until facilitators give them the floor. They convey their expertise articulately and precisely, and are concise in their expression. They also provide support to main speakers. They share the same opinion and fill in missing points. Under no circumstances do they make concessions in place of the main speakers. They listen attentively and object to demands or incorrect technical content from the other party.

The role of the observers: More than taking notes and keeping quiet

Interestingly, in the German-speaking region, the role of silent observers is rarely used, whereas in other cultural contexts, it's already the standard, such as in Asia. There, the silent observer is often also the most senior person. Before the negotiation, they receive the same briefing as other participants. What are silent observers' tasks during the negotiation? First and foremost, they listen and take notes. They do not actively participate and, at most, ask questions if something is not clear. They take notes using the "split sheet method" and record the following observations: exchanged information (interests/needs), the other party's initial demand, concessions from both sides in the correct order, possible solutions being developed. They can also signal to the facilitators when, in their estimation, there is a need for a break. What are silent observers' tasks during the breaks? They share the most important observations they have summarized, reporting objectively without criticizing colleagues. They also submit proposals and ideas for finding solutions.

VIRTUAL NEGOTIATION. BEST PRACTICE

The "split sheet method" has proven effective for keeping written records during virtual negotiations. This involves visually separating what you have said from what the other party has said, and comparing the two positions with each other. Try it during your next negotiation. It also works great on the phone.

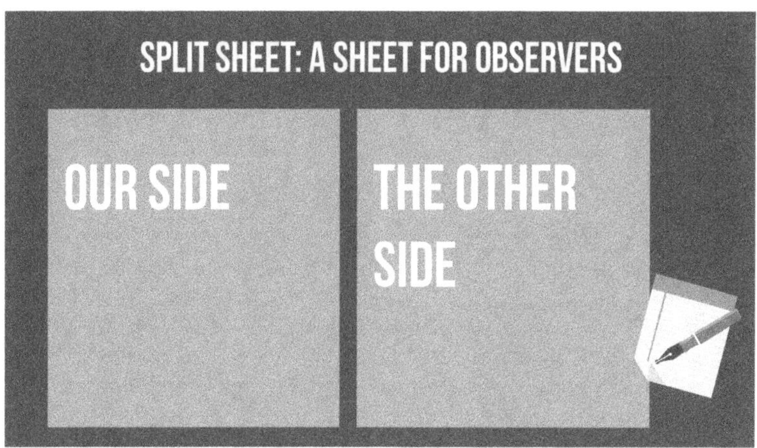

What are the benefits of taking notes in online negotiations? It's difficult to remember everything that was said if we don't put anything in writing. Agreements must also be written down so that we can refer to them in the future. The moment we write something down, we have the opportunity to slow down the pace of the virtual negotiation, to possibly follow up, and, later, to reflect based on the notes. In hindsight, it is much easier to analyze our actions when we have written records. It makes no difference whether each virtual negotiator takes notes individually, whether the person responsible for the minutes does it, or whether a shared document is used for this purpose. In the words of Winston Churchill: "A meeting is an event at which the minutes are kept and the hours are lost."

So, consider carefully who needs to participate in a virtual negotiation. Who do you actually need on the call, who should take on which role and why? Who can you afford to leave out? Who can you simply update afterwards? Who can assist and brief you in advance? Any individual who does not have an active role drains energy and momentum from an online negotiation. Why should I listen if I have no task? This is something the others will notice immediately and react to. One variation may be to work with part-time participants. For example, support speakers can be on standby and called in at the appropriate juncture. The legal department when it comes to legal aspects. The technicians when it comes to questions about operational issues. The salespeople when conditions are to be negotiated.

VIRTUAL NEGOTIATION. BEST PRACTICE

Less is more. Go through your own team's list of participants and filter out as many as you can. Limit the number of participants. As a rule of thumb, having more than eight negotiators drastically lowers the quality of the negotiation. Be sure to limit virtual negotiations to a maximum of ten people. However, don't forget to find out in advance how many people from the other party will be participating in the virtual negotiation in order to match or perhaps even trump their lineup.

VIRTUAL NEGOTIATION. TIP #4

The shorter the better: Limit the number of sessions

Every day we live with an overabundance of information. Thanks to the Internet, we have unlimited access to real-time news and background information. If a particular topic doesn't interest us, we quickly move on to the next one. Everything and everyone is competing for our attention, the real world with the virtual, and the virtual with the real. To avoid going crazy in this state of permanent sensory overload, we constantly filter and focus.

Continuous Partial Attention

American Linda Stone worked as a consultant for Apple and Microsoft Research before specializing in the publication of technical topics. As early as 1998, she coined the term CPA (Continuous Partial Attention) to describe what used to be an uncommon behavior of people, continuously dividing their attention. Stone claims that our motivation for doing this is rooted in our desire not to miss out on anything. If we are always on high alert, always ON, in a state of artificial alertness, then we continuously scan our surroundings, data, and facts. However, our attention lingers for only a very short time because we have already moved on to evaluating the next stimulus. Linda Stone emphasizes that CPA should not be confused with multitasking. Multitasking is when people strive to be more productive and efficient by doing multiple things at once. We answer an email while following a virtual meeting and eating a sandwich on the side. Strictly speaking, multitasking is merely a rapid switch between different activities. It just feels to us like we're doing multiple things at once.

The consequences resulting from CPA are manifold:

1. We perceive our lifestyle as stressful, as we feel we never get any rest.
2. We very often work in crisis management mode, because we are always tense.
3. We make quick concessions, even when it's necessary to think or decide thoroughly and creatively.
4. We feel overwhelmed and unfulfilled due to constant sensory overload since saying YES to one thing simultaneously means saying NO to many others.
5. We experience a sense of powerlessness because coping with the many stimuli leaves little time for action and creative endeavors.

The constant engagement with virtual stimuli and managing them affects the quality of human relationships. CPA can make it more difficult, especially online, to build a real connection with your negotiating parties. Negotiators you want to connect with are simultaneously engaged in scanning opportunities, activities, and news on social media while in a meeting with you, to avoid missing out. The longer a negotiation lasts, the greater the likelihood of distraction and the resulting lack of connection.

Gretchen Gavett, a Senior Editor at HBR (*Harvard Business Review*), summarized the result of the 2014 study, "What Employees Do During a Conference Call,"[8] by the U.S. company InterCall. Before the pandemic, InterCall was the leading provider of teleconferencing services and was used by 85 percent of the world's top 100 largest companies. Not only were the activities surprising, but the locations from which the conference participants dialed in were quite something:

1. "Outside grilling and getting a tan."
2. "In the tunnel that leads to NYC."
3. "At Disney World."
4. "In a dressing room, trying on clothes."
5. "In the closet of a friend's house during a party."
6. "On the beach... When the video call came in, I held my tablet up so my bikini didn't show."
7. "In the intensive care unit of a hospital."
8. "I was looking for my dog on the street because he had run away."

VIRTUAL NEGOTIATION. BEST PRACTICE

Long negotiations that work in an offline environment cannot be replicated one-to-one online. To keep attention high, it is significantly better to plan two online sessions of four hours or even shorter units for a negotiation that would have originally taken a full day. Ideally, you should structure individual sessions based on the negotiation process. Here's a suggestion for how a virtual negotiation with six individual sessions could look:

1st Session: Introduction/Topics/Challenges
2nd Session: Common and conflicting interests
3rd Session: Positions/Initial offer and counteroffer
4th Session: Enlarging the pie and developing creative approaches
5th Session: Negotiating the terms and concluding the deal
6th Session: Planning the implementation of the solution

VIRTUAL NEGOTIATION. TIP #5

Time to focus: Actively plan breaks

Just as important as limiting the number of participants and shortening the duration of virtual negotiations is taking regular breaks. During breaks, negotiators can relax, regenerate, and recharge their batteries. In a virtual setup, be sure to schedule regular breaks, at least every 60 to 90 minutes.

VIRTUAL NEGOTIATION. BEST PRACTICE

During breaks, virtual negotiators can mentally unwind and move around. It has proven effective to deliberately turn off cameras and sound. Make it a habit to double-check: Before leaving your workspace, ensure that the camera and audio are indeed turned off.

Zoom Fatigue

These days, one call follows the next, where previously you had meeting after meeting. There's no more travel time, no breaks, just a few clicks, and the thumbnails in front of you are filled with new faces and different topics. Exhaustion as a result of tightly scheduled virtual meetings and negotiations is common among online negotiators. First, one's concentration suffers, then negotiators become more irritable, until headaches and often sleep disturbances set in.

The Institute for Employment and Employability (IBE) in Ludwigshafen (IBE) conducted a comprehensive survey[9] in early September 2020. That was just over six months after the start of the pandemic, when companies and their employees had already become familiar with the technical execution of online meetings. Virtual communication and cooperation had become part of everyday life, and initial conclusions were drawn. In December 2020, a second phase of the survey followed to assess the developments.

Many respondents mentioned psychological symptoms. Only 15 to 30 percent of the respondents also showed physiological symptoms.

Psychological symptoms:

- Reduced concentration
- Restlessness
- Impatience
- Increased irritability
- Lack of balance
- Inappropriate behavior towards others
- Feeling annoyed

Physiological symptoms:

- Headaches
- Back pain

- Joint pain
- Stomach pain
- Sleep disturbances
- Visual disturbances

To counteract Zoom Fatigue and create the necessary conditions in virtual negotiations, it is essential to identify the causes. The survey identified three areas as stress factors: interpersonal aspects, organizational conditions, and technology.

Breaks help counteract excessive sobriety

More than two-thirds of respondents cited a lack of nonverbal feedback as a major stress factor, with a lack of small talk and reduced networking opportunities being particularly emphasized. Almost half of the respondents even explicitly criticized the lack of facial expressions and gestures, as a result of which meetings become more objective and soberer. Meeting participants desire more human warmth and time for socializing. Even in consideration of this aspect, well-rested negotiators are much better able to not only concentrate on the content of the virtual negotiation but also to dedicate a portion of their attention to the negotiation participants and their mood.

Breaks instead of a tight schedule of calls

The IBE study showed that the feeling of being rushed had already improved from September to December. Increased satisfaction was achieved by many companies and organizations deliberately scheduling breaks between calls and, in the case of longer meetings, during the actual meetings. Every virtual negotiator can remember this information when setting the agenda for a negotiation.

Breaks to recover from the use of technology

By now, employees have become accustomed to using technology for virtual communication. The sound and image quality, which was still experienced as burdensome at the beginning of the pandemic, is increasingly assessed as stable and therefore perceived as less burdensome. The same applies to the quality of Internet connections. Nevertheless, we sit in front of the screen for far too long. Mostly in a hunched posture, looking at the screen. Get up, stretch, do some breathing exercises, and do something good for your body.

"Go slow to go fast": Time to coordinate

Go slow to go fast? At first, that seems like a contradiction. In fact, however, it is highly beneficial to pause, reflect, and only then take action. This is true in the case of face-to-face negotiations and even more so for virtual ones, as it has become much easier to take breaks online. You can briefly coordinate with the negotiators from your own team in a side meeting, consult with supervisors or management, and then return to the main session. You can obtain opinions from experts and proceed with renewed knowledge.

"Go slow to go fast": Time for strategic planning

It is in the very nature of negotiation that we never have absolute transparency about what the other party really wants to achieve, and that we also do not reveal all our motives to the same extent. That means that it is inevitable that you will be confronted with new facts, motives, desires, and demands during a negotiation. And then what? This is the perfect time for a virtual break to evaluate the new information and adapt our strategy accordingly. In most cases, this break can also be sold as an advantage for the other party: "We have now made our offer and you have made your counteroffer. Shall we meet again in 30 minutes? This would allow us, as well as you, to review the offers and consider what the next steps might be."

"Go slow to go fast": Time to cool down

When emotions are running high and there is a risk of getting involved in a verbal spat, it is time to get out of action-reaction mode. Attacks become unobjective, and insults become personal. This in turn invites a tit-for-tat response, and we find ourselves in the middle of a dispute instead of a constructive negotiation. In this case, you may already be familiar with the recommendation from face-to-face negotiations to take a break and let your emotions settle down. The same applies to virtual negotiations. You could introduce a break in a friendly way with the words: "I feel we are going in circles. Have you also noticed how the tone has become more abrasive? I suggest we adjourn for half an hour and then resume the negotiation. Does that work for you as well?"

"Go slow to go fast": Time to include others

Negative emotions arise when people feel they have been excluded and left out. Especially in companies, it is often a matter of not leaving anyone out in the chain of information. Here, too, breaks in virtual negotiations can be supportive. A brief note to the relevant expert, supervisor, or partner will help you to get a thumbs-up from them when it's time to make a decision. "Give me a moment to get our supervisors on board. I'll get back to you in 15 minutes. Is that okay with you?" By involving the decision-makers early on, you avoid making decisions over their heads, which is something they both expect and appreciate. Another benefit of involving the right people is that they can make swift decisions, speeding up the overall negotiation process.

Go slow to go fast. Breaks are easier to take in a virtual setting than in face-to-face negotiations. They do not require extra space or travel. You can take advantage of breaks to briefly coordinate within your own team and to involve others early on rather than bypassing them. If things get heated, breaks provide a good opportunity to cool down. And if you receive a lot of new information that wasn't available to you beforehand, use breaks for strategic planning before making rash decisions.

VIRTUAL NEGOTIATION. TIP #6

Safety first! Minimize security risks

Nowadays it is easier than ever to record a negotiation. Any type of meeting can be recorded without difficulty using your smartphone, whether you are face-to-face, negotiating on the phone, or sitting in a video conference. Address before the virtual negotiation that no recordings or recordings of any kind may be made, so that any misunderstandings are cleared up in advance.

There are several ways to ensure a high degree of security:

1. A proper assessment and analysis of possible risks that takes place before the negotiation. If you are dealing with sensitive information, already consider the potential threats when preparing. Devise a plan to see if and how these can be reduced. Involve the IT department if there is uncertainty about which meeting software may be used. Try to create and send the meeting links, don't leave this step to the other party.

2. Establish a clear procedure regarding confidentiality. Non-disclosure agreements ensure that all parties involved are aware of the risks of security breaches, know the consequences of ignoring them, and know what to do in such a case. The signatories undertake to maintain confidentiality about negotiations, negotiation results, and confidential information.

VIRTUAL NEGOTIATION. KNOWLEDGE

What should be included in a confidentiality or non-disclosure agreement? In the global arena, non-disclosure agreements and confidential disclosure agreements are referred to as NDAs and CDAs, respectively. They are usually developed in close consultation with legal experts.

Possible elements of an NDA/CDA include:

- The names of the contracting parties (companies and persons)
- The specific information to be kept confidential, e.g. patents, licensing, intentions in mergers & acquisitions, RFLs (Requests for Information) or RFPs (Requests for Proposal)
- The information that is not to be treated as confidential
- The amount of possible penalties for breach of contract
- The duration of confidentiality

3. Comply with non-disclosure agreements and be consistent in taking action when they are violated. In this way, over time, a standard of compliance becomes established in companies and cultures as a fundamental way of engaging with one another. Compliance guidelines provide a clear and understandable description of the conduct that employees must observe towards customers and business partners. In many companies, they already form part of the Code of Conduct. You can also always address how important

it is to follow this rule. In this way, confidentiality becomes a basic principle that applies online just as much as it does in person.

4. Offer training. All parties involved in a negotiation are trained on what the terms of the NDA are, how to identify security risks, and what they can and must do if they detect security holes.

5. Ensure a secure environment. Online negotiations are not to be conducted in public. Not on the train, not in the lounge at the airport, and not in the car on the phone when going on vacation with the family. Always protect your data on your laptop in public with a privacy filter, through which only you can see your screen. Anyone else, including colleagues, strangers, or competitors, will only see a black screen should they take a look. Close the door to your office when you're conferencing online, or retreat to an undisturbed room.

6. Develop a backup plan and designate the person responsible for digital security. Large companies have safety officers. These safety officers handle digital as well as non-digital security. Include them in important negotiations in good time. They can even take part in online negotiations with high prestige value to always keep an eye on digital security. Active negotiators are often busy with so many other things that they are grateful when an expert deals with this issue.

7. Record exactly which agreements, especially with regard to confidentiality, have been made during the online negotiation. Also document your concerns or any violations immediately. This could be important for later legal disputes.

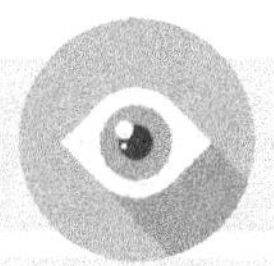

In Chapter 3, "Well-Equipped from the Start," you learned how important it is to carefully prepare your online negotiations, and got to know six tips. What specific suggestions do you take away from the individual tips?

Tip #1: Decide first! Auction or negotiation? Virtual or in person?

....

Tip #2: The new way to prepare for a negotiation is much like the negotiation process itself

....

 Tip #3: Less is more: Limit the number of participants

....

Tip #4: The shorter the better: Limit the number of sessions

....

Tip #5: Time to focus: Actively plan breaks

....

Tip #6: Safety first: Minimize security risks

....

CHAPTER 4. So Close and Yet So Far – Communication in Remote Negotiations

In the morning, you discussed the current delivery delays with suppliers in Southeast Asia. Only half of the participants in this online meeting had their cameras on, and the others were also very quiet. An hour later, you pass the information on to your own team so that the customer can be informed. In the background, you constantly hear the clacking of the keyboard, while the eyes of your colleagues are wandering around the screen. You can tell that they are doing something else! In the afternoon, a young employee wants to negotiate with you whether he can work from home more often. He has just finished his apprenticeship and started work during the lockdown. You haven't really warmed to him yet.

Perhaps you have experienced days like this. Or similar ones. We can connect with negotiating parties all over the world with just one click. We bring them into our office or even into our home. We can have many such negotiations in a single day. And although this brings us very close to other people, we often feel so far away from one another.

In this chapter, we explore the topics of "Getting in touch" and "Keeping in touch," because many virtual negotiators feel that it is more difficult to get in touch online. And just as many negotiators are concerned with how to stay in touch in an appropriate way. Even making small talk online is uncomfortable for many people. Why? Because you are literally "confronted" with technology and always have to see yourself in miniature on the screen, which inhibits many people. On the next few pages, you'll get tips on which topics are suitable for digi-chats and which ones you'd better not address. In order to conduct virtual negotiations most efficiently, it can be helpful to establish a set of rules for communication and to summarize the conversation again and again. This is also possible without it coming across as overly preachy or contrived.

We will also clarify the question of whether there are differences in communication between external or internal partners and why internal team communication is sometimes even more challenging.

Getting in touch – Keeping in touch

Negotiation is impossible without communication, neither in online nor in face-to-face negotiations. If parties do not interact with each other in some way, negotiations cannot take place. The manner in which negotiators interact with one another determines whether proposals are made, compromises are found, and agreements are reached at a later stage. Communication can either create obstacles or break them down. Latent biases can be confirmed or overcome. Trust, openness, and cooperation can occur in the same way as mistrust, suspicion, and entrenchment. Once the dogs have been let off the leash and aggression starts to build, they may start to bite each other, and it will be difficult to get them back on the leash and calm them down. Only by remaining calm and collected are negotiators able to communicate professionally. This applies to virtual negotiations to the same, if not to a greater, extent.

One of the world's most renowned negotiation experts is Gavin Kennedy, Professor Emeritus at Heriot-Watt University in Edinburgh, who not only wrote the bestseller *Everything is Negotiable. How to get the Best Deal Every Time*[10], but also a whopping eleven books on the subject. According to Kennedy, the percentage of communication in a face-to-face negotiation is about 85 percent.[11] Hereunder he defines the following aspects of communication: making small talk, answering questions that have been posed to us, making statements about a particular topic, summarizing our understanding, and expressing criticism. We only make specific suggestions about ten percent of the negotiation time, and five percent of that time is spent attempting to reach an agreement. On this basis, he recommends that virtual negotiators take an in-depth look at communication. A virtual negotiation professional is also always a communication professional.

The early bird catches the worm: Start building good relationships early on

Even well in advance, online negotiators can do a lot to build relationships. The more often we have contact with a person, the more likeable we usually find them. Therefore, use as many communication channels as possible, from social media platforms to a quick confirmation or a thank-you-for-the-info email. It is better to pick up the phone once in a while than to always write emails, so that you have heard your counterpart in person and, in the best case, seen them once during a short video call.

Gradually identify common ground

Seek out and find common ground. Often it takes a little time, sometimes it happens very quickly. Negotiators who have many things in common believe they are similar to one another. This creates trust. Even if you are not one of the lucky ones who have already met their negotiating parties in person, be sure to look for similarities and commonalities. Maybe you are from the same state, graduated from the same college, have the same hobby, or have children the same age. Also, don't be afraid to take a look at the LinkedIn profile in advance or to do some quick research on the Internet. You may have common contacts or common areas of professional interest.

Keep at it

After you have invested time and effort into building good relationships with your online negotiators, the key is to stay on the ball. Always remember: It is up to you what image your negotiating parties have of you. As the German saying goes, in life we see each other twice, only sometimes the second time is the first time we see a person face-to-face.

Try this:

- Formulate friendly and personal emails (Tip: Begin with the matter at hand, followed by the niceties ☺).
- Follow your contact on professional social media channels (LinkedIn, XING).
- Stay up to date on the current issues faced by the negotiating parties (industry, company, area).
- Send birthday greetings.

VIRTUAL NEGOTIATION. BEST PRACTICE

In online negotiations, a person's primal, predisposed communication behavior can sometimes be reinforced. Introverts are even less likely to engage in extensive small talk. Extroverts also take up a lot of space online and need to be reeled in gently from time to time. Remember that negotiators from other cultures also act differently in terms of their communication style: Online negotiators from cultures with a more direct negotiation style will get to the point even faster and feel they are very efficient in doing so. Online negotiators from cultures with an indirect negotiation style will be even less open, especially in the case of negative decisions, and may prefer to sit out one or two.

BETTINA KAPPE

Bettina Kappe has a degree in psychology and business administration. The experienced senior consultant has been teaching negotiation skills for many years in the international environment of large corporations.

J.P. Bettina, you have already negotiated a lot with various target groups such as other managers, supervisors, and the works council as head of the department for personnel development. Today, your training and coaching repertoire includes negotiation as one of its main focuses. From a psychologist's perspective, what are the biggest challenges in virtual negotiation?

B.K. Body language is limited in the digital realm. By now, it has become customary to at least always turn on the camera. However, if your partner's connection is poor or there are larger groups negotiating, then at times you won't be able to see anyone, which represents a loss of information. Another challenge is initiating the establishment of rapport, which is often shorter in a digital context, and the limited body language, which can make building the relationship more difficult.

J.P. The time limit for virtual negotiations is often one hour with MS Teams or Zoom. In contrast, in face-to-face negotiations, a buffer is usually built in, and afterwards the negotiators go out for coffee or a meal together. What does this time limitation result in?

B.K. Often, at the next meeting, you have to start all over again. The interruption makes it much more difficult for virtual negotiators to get into the flow. If we look at the importance of relationships in psychology, then getting in touch in the digital space has become more difficult. When I think about Cialdini's Principles of Influence, more work needs to be done here, much better listening is required, and attention to language is essential.

J.P. You always emphasize how helpful it is to be well-equipped in terms of technology so that sound, light, and background look professional. What tips do you have from the therapist's perspective besides having smoothly functioning technology for online negotiations?

B.K. Just like in my solution-oriented coaching sessions, I try to make virtual negotiators more aware of language and questioning techniques. Slowing down and not going too fast, especially in the beginning, is important to avoid being rushed by the time frame and making mistakes as a result.

J.P. Known advantages of virtual negotiation, which you also mention in your training, are that you can save travel costs and time, along with other resources, such as room bookings, catering, energy costs, etc. Additionally, the flexibility (location, independence, cross-border, etc.) has increased. Are there any other advantages?

B.K. I am convinced that virtual negotiations are more efficient if they are well prepared. Virtual negotiation is often much more focused, due to digital time frames and deadlines. With larger groups, there is less participation with digressive comments or input, which also increases the pace.

J.P. Bettina, you talk about it being easier to negotiate virtually when the parties involved already know each other. What if this is not the case?

B.K. Then I recommend that virtual negotiators meet in person whenever possible to get to know each other. It's a worthwhile investment in the relationship.

Here you can learn more about
Bettina Kappe.

Here you can learn more about
Robert Cialdini.

The talent of professional persuasion

When people talk about the way negotiators communicate, there is sometimes confusion about whether it is the art of negotiation or the power of persuasion that inspires success. What is the difference? The Huthwaite International Institute is one of the world's leading institutes specializing in sales and negotiation training. According to a 2014 Huthwaite study titled[12] "How well are you negotiating?" the difference is that in a negotiation, both parties communicate with each other to come together and find a solution, while persuasion is a process carried out by only one party. The Englishman Richard Mullender[13], a negotiation instructor for difficult negotiations with hostage-takers at Scotland Yard, reinforces this view. Negotiating with hostage-takers is a one-way process, in his opinion. There is never any question of agreeing to the demands of the other party, let alone compromising with criminals.

A negotiator's goal is to persuade the other party to take an action that is in the negotiator's interest. As a negotiator, it is important that you know when it's the right time to persuade. This will always be the case if you disagree with the other party. Now the question arises of how to persuade in a professional manner. Successful negotiators, according to the Huthwaite International Institute study cited earlier, proceed as follows: Surprisingly, the other party is first asked to present their point of view. This is followed by a series of clarifying questions to gain a deeper understanding of the other person's point of view. Only then do successful negotiators persuade the other person of their stance. They understand that presenting one's opinion too early rarely persuades anyone. Richard Mullender confirms this approach based on his Scotland Yard experience. It is very promising to try to change the minds of hostage-takers. Rather, he always tries to understand their opinions in greater detail so that he can use them against the criminals to achieve the desired result.

VIRTUAL NEGOTIATION. TIP #8

Making small talk online

Small talk is to an online negotiation as an appetizer is to a good meal. In many cultures, building a lasting relationship is seen as the most important part of negotiation. Small talk is part of business, whether you like it or not. Once you start to trust one another, contractual issues are often no more than a formality. Be sure to ask lots of open questions to encourage your negotiating parties to reveal something about themselves. The answers to closed questions are only "yes" or "no."

Tips on how to make small talk in online negotiations:

1. Demonstrate genuine interest by listening carefully and responding to what you are told.
2. Also share personal experiences online with small anecdotes from your own life that are appropriate to the situation. Show the others who you are.
3. As the conversation progresses, focus on the common threads and thereby weave the narrative into a strong bond.
4. Keep the small talk light. Small talk is like a little white cloud in the sky, not a storm cloud. Heavy, controversial, and negative topics don't make you want to keep talking.
5. Be present. Give your virtual negotiation partners your full attention. Avoid distractions, no matter how tempting it may be to take a quick peek at your inbox.
6. Show empathy. Look for emotional reactions, recognize them even in small talk, and mirror your counterpart's affectedness.
7. Humorous small talk is permitted. It has been proven that laughing together raises the spirits. Of course it's better to make fun of yourself than of others.
8. Focus on what is positive and upbeat. Reinforce the positives and leave the negatives aside. This already sets the tone for the upcoming negotiation.

Topics that are suitable for virtual small talk:

- Whether online or not – the weather remains the classic par excellence
- The occasion of the negotiation – topicality of the issue
- The city, region, or country in which the negotiating parties live
- Current news – make sure you only discuss positive news
- Regulations on remote working in the respective organization
- Vacation destinations – very popular especially during the vacation season

- Hobbies – everyone likes to talk about their interests, why not dig deeper with a few questions

Topics to avoid when making virtual small talk:

- Controversial topics, such as politics or religion
- Personal issues, such as health problems or financial difficulties
- Topics that are too private, such as details about intimate relationships
- Offensive and sensitive topics, such as sexist or racist comments

VIRTUAL NEGOTIATION. BEST PRACTICE

Do you have a mutual contact? Someone your new business partners and you both trust? Wonderful! At the beginning of the first virtual get-to-know-you session, ask this person to take on the role of host and introduce you to each other. This works like a turbocharger for building trust, especially when it's not yourself but others who speak positively about you.

VIRTUAL NEGOTIATION. TIP #9

Establishing the rules of communication

Time and again, overlapping contributions to the conversation which come in with a time delay impede the flow of negotiations and thoughts. In addition, fewer communication signals are available to us in online negotiations. Unfortunately, this leaves more room for interpretation and speculation as to how things are meant. Clear rules of communication can help to some extent. Here, the question is:

- How do I address the rules of communication appropriately ?
- What kind of communication rules help to achieve better results in online negotiations?
- When should I bring up the rules for communication?
- When should I not bring up the rules for communication?

How do I address the rules of communication appropriately ?

If you are satisfied with the tone and efficiency of previous negotiations, you do not need to establish ground rules. Experienced virtual negotiators are familiar with the "instruction manual" for effective communication from each of their online meetings. Online conferences have long since become the new normal, and participants are now largely familiar with the rules of constructive communication. However, if negotiators are unfamiliar with the rules of communication, the question arises as to when and how this is addressed and what rules are necessary.

However, proclaiming rules with a raised index finger or indirectly addressing the misconduct of the negotiating parties will not win you any sympathy points. In the best case, you will be met with a frown; in the worst case, you will be met with open hostility. Therefore, think carefully about what rules of communication you really want to establish. *Less is more* also applies to the rules of communication. Use your intuition to choose what will really increase the effectiveness. Sometimes it is not such a big deal to interrupt or be interrupted when the whole negotiation team is in the flow. Sell the rules of communication as a win-win for everyone involved and provide the reasons why. Present them as a suggestion. Remain open to additions and adjustments. Get the approval of all parties involved.

What kind of rules for communication help to achieve better results in online negotiations?

1. We communicate clearly and concisely. We clearly share our intentions and needs. We avoid ambiguity and room for interpretation.
2. We actively listen to and focus on what others are saying. We think before we answer.
3. We treat each other with respect, even if we don't agree with one another. We do not attack each other personally and do not insult each other.
4. We focus on the matter at hand and have our emotions under control. We are neither overly aggressive nor passive.
5. We respond immediately. We respond quickly to emails or messages and avoid long waiting times.
6. We document the outcome and all related messages of the online negotiation for future reference.
7. Any party may wish to interrupt the online negotiation at any time, especially if tempers are running high. We will continue virtual negotiations only when all sides have calmed down.

When should I bring up the rules for communication?

At the beginning of the virtual negotiation, address the way in which you want talk to each other if you know from previous experience that communication is sometimes problematic. Suggest rules of communication during the virtual negotiation if you feel the negotiation has stalled or is about to escalate because major communication blunders are impeding the overall tone, process, or work towards an outcome.

When should I not bring up the rules for communication?

In a virtual negotiation with external customers, it would seem very strange if you started the online negotiation with a set of rules. The same applies to all situations in which the negotiating power is distributed to your disadvantage. A supplier in a monopolistic situation does not want to be reprimanded. The start-up with which you are exploring the possibilities of potential collaboration would be puzzled by these initial steps. Internally, the situation is similar. In asymmetric internal relationships, addressing rules for communication at the outset is not appropriate. Your supervisor would frown, as would the management board, if you as an employee were to rush ahead too quickly.

VIRTUAL NEGOTIATION. TIP #10

Summarizing. Summarizing. Summarizing!

Your morning is crammed with appointments, with one online meeting following the next. You've got a quick lunch, and then it's off to the next negotiation of a more complex nature. You don't feel 100 percent confident in your expertise. The midday slump does the rest. Many of you may be familiar with similar situations. And sometimes you're sitting in a negotiation and feel like your mental capacity has already been maxed out. If you're looking for an easy-to-use communication tool that virtual negotiators can use to help themselves and others at such crucial moments, try summarizing. Do it often and over and over again. Not only at the end, but also in between. This signals that you are listening and want to understand. It shows the negotiating parties that you have listened to what they have to say and that you understand what is important to the other party. This reflects to the other party that you are all ears and at the same time allows you to check whether you have really grasped the context completely. At the end, send a summarizing email.

What intellectual skills characterize professional summarizing?

1. Understanding the main interests and positions of both sides
2. The retention of the associated arguments
3. The omission of unnecessary information and details
4. "Getting to the point" through precise phrasing and writing
5. Quick comprehension, classification, and interpretation of facts and the motives of the negotiators
6. High attention to detail, accuracy, and due diligence
7. The ability to recognize patterns and relationships
8. The knowledge of the relevant vocabulary and corresponding terms

According to the Huthwaite International study mentioned earlier, skilled negotiators spend 17.2 percent of negotiation time assessing their understanding of the situation, while average negotiators spend only 8.3 percent. If your summary is thorough, it confirms to the negotiators that you have really listened to them and that they have been understood. If something is still missing, the other party has the opportunity to add it. The amount of effort required to utilize summarizing as a tool is low. The payoff, on the other hand, is high. From time to time, however, there may be negotiators who actually believe that just because you have listened properly and really understood, you will automatically agree to their demands. "Nothing is agreed until everything is agreed" is a negotiating credo from the Americans. Address this misunderstanding openly right away. "I have understood what you expect. However, that does not mean that we have already reached an agreement."

Leading virtually by summarizing

Another not to be underestimated aspect of summarization is to steer the conversation back to the agenda. It occasionally happens that virtual negotiators get lost in discussions about details or get side-tracked. Summarizing is a handy tool to elegantly refocus on the actual agenda. "Let's take a look at where we are right now. We have already agreed together that ... If you agree, we will take it one step further. We now arrive at the following question ..."

Tips for phrasing when summarizing orally in virtual negotiations:

- "Let me briefly summarize what I have understood ..."
- "Correct me if I'm wrong. What I'm hearing is that you're particularly concerned that ..."
- "So, you're saying that ... Am I understanding this right?"
- "Okay, let me quickly recap what I've understood. You still have concerns that ..."

What is the purpose of written summaries?

The added value of summarizing an online negotiation is to help you and others sift through all the important details even after the virtual negotiation has ended and to be able to recall them as needed. This enables customers, suppliers, and employees who were unable to attend the negotiations to find out what happened and what was agreed on. At the same time, a summarizing email following an online negotiation serves as a reference for later discussions.

How do you summarize an online negotiation?

1. Take detailed notes during the negotiation.
2. Use a highlighter to emphasize the most important statements while you are still negotiating.
3. Make a note of questions and objections in the margin so that you don't forget to follow up.
4. Highlight important decisions with color.
5. Share the summary with all parties immediately following the virtual negotiation.

6. Also send the summary to other parties involved, without artificially inflating the distribution list.

7. Don't forget to allocate tasks to individual people and provide them with a timeline.

8. Attach additional files if that was agreed upon.

Ensure internal team communication

This tip is one of the most important. Why? Because many virtual negotiators do not see the need to ensure internal team communication during an online negotiation, although this is quite easy and offers many advantages. If you and your team work remotely, communication within your own team may be somewhat restricted. In the past, negotiators used to communicate regularly and intensively during the preparation phase. They would briefly consult with each other during breaks in negotiations or step out for lunch to go over details. Today, much of that has ceased to exist. How do you implement a tactical break nowadays? How do you strategically coordinate with one another during a negotiation?

Set up a second communication channel. Under no circumstances should you use the chat function of your video conferencing system for this purpose, as this can easily lead to errors and confusion. All it takes is one wrong click and your counterpart will receive internal information that was not intended for them. You can set up a second internal team channel using an online messenger service such as Slack or a WhatsApp group chat on your cell phone. This allows you to stay in contact during the virtual negotiation and exchange information at any time without the other party noticing.

VIRTUAL NEGOTIATION. TIP #12

Have the courage to also show your emotions virtually

People learn to control their emotions from an early age. What is permitted for children is seen as socially unwelcome and inappropriate for adults. Negative emotions such as anger, frustration, and sadness are not exhibited in public. The supervisor who rages and yells at their employees is ridiculed. The employee who complains because they have too much work is not taken very seriously. The working atmosphere in our culture is characterized by something resembling sterile objectivity. There is no room for feelings; they are considered to be a hindrance. We also hold back from openly showing positive emotions, such as joy, in public. In the Huthwaite International Study, negotiators were asked whether they would express their negative emotions, such as "I am disappointed by your response." Only 20 percent of all negotiators reported expressing any feelings at all in the workplace. True negotiation professionals, however, did it significantly more often, according to Huthwaite International. This is surprising, because the common belief is still that real negotiation experts have a poker face and do not show any emotional reactions. Huthwaite International recommends that negotiators allow their emotions. Let's assume that in a price negotiation there are different opinions about the amount of the offer. As long as negotiators only dispute the amount of the offer through argumentation, an exchange of arguments can last as long as they want. However, if one of the negotiators expresses their disappointment, it becomes more challenging for the other party not to acknowledge it and thus reject the offer. Phrases in which negotiators express their own feelings, such as "I have doubts," "I'm concerned about...," "I feel troubled by...," or "I'm not sure how to respond to this," come across as authentic because they demonstrate the negotiator's degree of affectedness. Obviously, it's easier to express positive feelings. When you communicate negative feelings, it's essential to make sure to keep those feelings with yourself and not project them onto the other party or blame them for them. There is a gender stereotype that women are more likely than men to talk about how they feel. Interestingly, this has not been confirmed for women's behavior in negotiations. According to Huthwaite International, there were no significant differences between the sexes. However, it was observed the frequency with which emotions were allowed increased with age. Huthwaite International assumes that increasing maturity allows a person to overcome the restrictions of childhood (suppressing feelings).

VIRTUAL NEGOTIATION. BEST PRACTICE

Especially in online negotiations, discussions are often even more matter-of-fact and objective than in face-to-face negotiations. Therefore, it's important to express your personal degree of affectedness in words. This makes you appear more human and credible. Conversely, also listen carefully when negotiators from the other party share how they feel.

 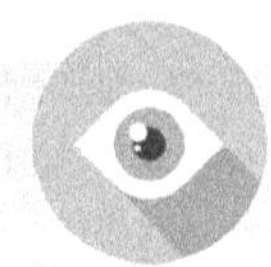

In Chapter 4, the tagline was "So Close and Yet So far!" You received six tips for good communication in remote negotiations. Take a few minutes and think about what specific ideas you will take away from this chapter:

Tip #7: Getting in touch – Keeping in touch

....

Tip #8: Making small talk online

....

Tip #9: Establishing the rules of communication

....

Tip #10: Summarizing. Summarizing. Summarizing!

....

Tip #11: Internal team communication

....

Tip #12: Have the courage to also show your emotions virtually

....

CHAPTER 5. Making the Most of It – Overcoming Limitations in Body Language

We can probably all agree that one of the biggest differences between virtual and face-to-face negotiation is that we cannot not truly experience the other person in 3D and up close. We never know for sure how the other negotiating parties are reacting to our proposal: do they agree, are they still hesitant, or have they had a negative attitude right from the outset? We pick up a large part of this information intuitively via the non-verbal reaction of our counterpart. In a real room we can see most of our negotiator's body. In face-to-face negotiations the table represents the subject of the negotiation: if someone pushes documents, a glass, a coffee cup, or a pen forward, the person is very likely to support our offer. If the negotiating parties withdraw something, they are likely not in agreement. Alas, things used to be much simpler with face-to-face negotiations. Online we can only capture fragments of these clear signals. Let us therefore consider how the limitations of body language can be overcome. It is helpful to understand why it is important to turn on the camera, what the obstacles there are, and how to overcome them. You will learn how to position yourself most advantageously in front of the camera and what role the appropriate light plays so that you are not sitting in the dark. Even though we are not able to observe quite as much and quite as accurately as in face-to-face negotiations, some interesting information can be extracted from the reactions of the negotiating parties.

Don't speak into the void: Turn your camera on

After two years of a pandemic, even the last holdouts can't help but accept the hard truth: For the rest of their working lives, they will have to live with the fact that the camera on their screen is not just a meaningless ornament used by self-absorbed influencers to upload touched-up videos to Instagram. They themselves will have to turn on the camera when participating in video calls. This comes easily to extroverts. However, introverts have to overcome their fears to do so. Fortunately, there are coping strategies to deal with this unfamiliar and, for some, scary situation.

Why so many virtual negotiators don't like to turn on the camera

There are surprisingly many "quiet" people, often technicians and engineers, who believe that virtual meetings drain their energy. Even just having a camera turned on is experienced somewhat like being in the spotlight. It takes energy, and not much energy comes back through these terribly small thumbnails; they only increase the tension and discomfort. What can introverts and camera-shy people do to avoid missing out and being left behind for years to come? First and foremost, let's be honest: Is it perhaps only the very significant online meetings and virtual negotiations with a large budget that trigger fear? Aren't many of the "quiet" people often quite brave when it comes to the jour-fix, virtual preparation meetings, and one-on-ones? That would be good, as it's something they can work with and practice. They can use small negotiations as a training ground for the bigger ones.

The good news is that there are pretty simple means by which we all can calm our minds and bodies in the face of a computer camera. First answer the following questions:[14]

- What do I already have under control?
- To whom or to what am I giving my attention?
- What kind of meeting culture do we have?
- How can I arm myself against moods of hostility?

If you don't like turning on the camera, consider what the problem might be. Why exactly do you find it more comfortable without a camera? Do you suffer from impostor syndrome and occasionally feel like you're not good enough in other situations as well? Are you pressed for time right now and think more time would have been necessary to prepare properly? Do you generally prefer to stay in the background? Or do you just not like the sound of your voice or the way you look on the screen? Maybe you had a bad WIFI connection during the last virtual negotiation, and without a camera the connection was more stable?

What do I already have under control?

If you answer the question of what you already have under control, you will see that it is quite a bit. This will also make you aware of your self-efficacy.

VIRTUAL NEGOTIATION. KNOWLEDGE

Self-efficacy
The concept of self-efficacy refers to the confidence we have in ourselves to act as we wish, even in extreme situations, based on our own competencies. Canadian psychologist Albert Bandura, who taught at Stanford University, is considered an important proponent of social cognitive learning theory. He found that people can influence their personal behavior. We can be self-organizing, proactive, as well as self-reflective and self-regulating. Based on

this observation, Bandura created the concept of self-efficacy in the 1980s. People are capable of making a difference with their behaviors and choices. In the absence of self-efficacy, there is a feeling of having no control and of being determined by external circumstances. Self-efficacy always comes with the question: "Can I really do this?" It can be learned and trained. Professor Bandura identified four different factors from which self-efficacy can arise:

1. Having positive experiences
2. Seeking out role models
3. Allowing yourself to be encouraged
4. Controlling your emotions

However, in dealing with your camera shyness, you will also identify things that are out of your control. You will only be able to influence the quality of the bandwidth to a limited extent and only partially affect the reactions of the negotiating parties. But you can make sure you're set up with a good camera, a quality microphone, excellent lighting, and a suitable background. Once you hear your voice and see yourself, you'll start to feel much more comfortable.

If you know you're in for a week of especially camera-intensive negotiations, you should already schedule fixed periods of downtime before the negotiations start. Invest 15 minutes to mentally wrap up the last topic. This will help you prepare and focus for your next virtual negotiation. Review your schedule and block out time slots between online negotiations well in advance.

To whom or to what am I giving my attention?

Behind the reluctance to turn on the camera may also lie the pressure to perform, perfectionism, self-doubt, and a lack of self-confidence. If you increasingly focus your attention on how you are perceived by others and constantly interpret the facial expressions of the negotiating parties, then that is where your attention lies. If you are constantly checking yourself, being very strict with yourself, and thinking about how you could have worded something better, then you are focusing too much on yourself. This is exhausting and stressful. Our brain sends signals to our nervous system that danger is imminent. Stress hormones are released. Our breathing picks up, and we start talking faster. We begin to sweat, our muscles tense up, and we prepare to flee or attack. Formulating clever thoughts becomes more difficult.

The good news is that we can break free from this cycle of stress. High-performance athletes use mental training to avoid being dominated by stress reactions. They learn to use conscious breathing as a tool for regulation. It also helps to take a deep breath before the online negotiation. In addition, prolonging exhalation leads to a slowing of the heartbeat. For many people, leaning back in their chair or sitting up helps. Even a short-term redirection of attention objects that are associated with calm and positive memories or the use a stress ball can help with stress reduction. Looking at a cherished family photo or holding a seashell that you picked up at the North Sea during your last summer vacation can bring peace and relaxation.

VIRTUAL NEGOTIATION. KNOWLEDGE

Self-regulation
Self-regulationis a collective term used in psychology to describe people's ability to control their attention, emotions, impulses, and actions. It encompasses dealing with one's own feelings and moods. Self-regulation training aims to reduce excessively high emotional levels through relaxation or to increase a too low emotional level through mobilization. Unfamiliar situations are often accompanied by excessive arousal. This state of arousal can be influenced and specifically reduced through breathing exercises and relaxation techniques.

If we succeed in directing our focus on one of these things, we can become physically calmer, and our conscious thinking will return to the forefront. The danger with fear is to fall into intuitive behavior. However, if you implement one tip after another – controlling your breathing and body, leaning back in your chair, and focusing on your attention points like a photo or a souvenir – then the sum of these small activities becomes a foundation that serves as a source of calm and strength for you.

What kind of meeting culture do we have?

How vulnerable is your company or organization to last-minute or disorganized online negotiations? If you are responsible for a virtual negotiation, you should

- send an invitation in advance,
- set an agenda,
- be clear about what the goal of the virtual negotiation is and
- who is playing which role in this particular negotiation,
- ensure that each participant knows the strategy, and
- that adequate time has been allotted for the virtual negotiation.

You should even think about whether an official online negotiation is actually necessary or if an email exchange could suffice. Maybe a short phone call will do the trick. In a nutshell: Virtual negotiations with a camera are not always the best form of communication.

If virtual negotiations are convened too often, at too short notice, and unnecessarily, it is very difficult to prepare adequately. In particular, employees who work from home tend to change roles much more frequently than those at work, even within the same day. For example, they may have to prepare a snack for their children, quickly turn on the washing machine, or take the dog for a walk around the block. People working alone from an office at home are often more concerned about an upcoming virtual negotiation. At the office, people have the opportunity to discuss things with colleagues over a coffee beforehand and exchange ideas.

There are five ways you can deal with poor planning:

- 1st Change the meeting culture within your organization and talk about how negotiators benefit when they have enough time to prepare for a virtual negotiation.
- 2nd Demand discipline from others and, if necessary, cancel your participation if you have the authority to do so. Continuously point out that the quality of the results of virtual negotiations increases with good preparation.
- 3rd Make a weekly schedule and build in time buffers for the unexpected. Use these time blocks to prepare for online negotiations that have been scheduled on short notice.
- 4th Block out one or two days per week for quiet conceptual work – these are the times when you can devote yourself entirely to preparing for virtual negotiations. The other three days of the week are "camera days." This is when your hair is in place, makeup is on point, and your shirt is ironed.
- 5th At the beginning of the week, ask yourself which of the virtual negotiations are of the most importance to you, and do a pre-check-in to calm yourself down: Before officially dialing in check the technology, the light and the function of the link for your online negotiation.

How do I arm myself against moods of hostility?

Difficult conversations in a hostile atmosphere are often perceived as more unpleasant on camera than in face-to-face negotiations. As nonverbal cues are harder to read, online negotiators start to interpret more heavily and make wild assumptions. Sometimes a phone call can even be easier because you don't even begin to look for and interpret hidden signals. If you have a very difficult on-camera negotiation coming up, here's how you can prepare for it: Think of a person who makes you feel completely safe and loved, like a good friend, partner, or even your child or a pet. Then associate the face, look, laugh, voice, or touch of that familiar person or animal with the anxiety-producing situation. This positive affirmation calms your nervous system. As soon as you stop ruminating, your fear of the situation diminishes. If your schedule permits, it also helps to make a phone call asking your loved one to be with you in spirit as you kick off the negotiation and turn on the camera. You may even have time before the challenging virtual negotiation to go to lunch with a pal, which will allow you to take some of the positive energy with you into the conversation. Using gratitude to help you is also simple and valuable. And last but not least: Even if online negotiations with a camera are stressful for you, remind yourself of the basic advantages of virtual negotiation.

Why we don't like speaking into the void

Few things captivate us more than a human face. Studies have shown that toddlers look twice as long at simplified human faces as they do at shapes. We achieve most of our effect on others through non-verbal communication, such as facial expressions, gestures, body posture, and voice. To avoid remaining just a disembodied voice, it is recommended to turn on your camera in virtual negotiations and to be visible to the negotiating parties. However, an unpleasant situation can quickly arise if we have the camera on but are only looking into the void ourselves. They can see us, but we can't see them. It's very irritating. We don't get a response to what we say. How can we get the negotiating parties in online negotiations to turn on their camera as well?

VIRTUAL NEGOTIATION. QR

Here you can find out which webcams performed best out of 21 tested models on chip.de in May 2022.

It all starts with the invitation. This is sent in advance via email to the participants of the online negotiation. In addition to the list of participants and the agenda you can also include the "Netiquette." A few kind words about how you would like participants to conduct themselves during the virtual negotiation. Turning on one's camera is part of having good manners. If there is a generally respectful atmosphere, it is also sufficient to send a message expressing your excitement to see the negotiating parties.

VIRTUAL NEGOTIATION. KNOWLEDGE

Netiquette
"Netiquette" refers to proper and respectful behavior in virtual communication. The aim of netiquette is to create a manner of communication that is pleasant for all participants. In online negotiations, it is important to consider the following points:

Interpersonal
Address your counterparts by their names. Make sure that the participants agree on the form of address. There are cultural differences here. In France, for example, people consistently address one another formally, whereas in the Anglo-American cultural area and in the international business world, the use of first names is common. Furthermore, as in face-to-face meetings, rudeness, personal attacks, innuendos, and discriminatory remarks against minorities are not allowed.

Technology
Even before the online negotiation, familiarize yourself with the key features of the platform being used. Negotiators should know how to share a presentation, where the chat function is located, and how to turn the microphone and camera on and off.

Legibility
Correct sentence structure and spelling (including capitalization); use visible quotation marks for citing without altering the wording;

eliminate unnecessary information; avoid excessive formatting and the overuse of colors; writing in ALL CAPS or continuous **bold text** is considered aggressive and should be avoided. Furthermore, it is considered impolite to string together multiple punctuation marks like this!!!!

Subject and text in emails

To ensure that the content of emails can be quickly understood, categorized, and properly filed, the subject should be informative and clear. Write two emails rather than incorporating too many topics into one message. Use short sentences and avoid abbreviations and technical terms that the other negotiating parties might not be familiar with.

Confidentiality

It is best to conceal what is not intended for third parties, as you do not know who else will read an email. Remember: emails are for eternity. Sometimes it is better to have a confidential phone conversation.

Legal issues

In Germany, copyright, image rights, and quotation rights must be observed. Other countries may have different laws. Inquire about any legal specifics in advance.

Chat

This is where netiquette becomes chatiquette. Write only short messages in the chat and do not forget that most of the time the person leading the online negotiation has to keep an eye on this communication channel in addition to coordinating the negotiation. This is an additional task that requires a great deal of concentration, so some messages may go unnoticed.

Reactions

Sending hearts, applauding, giving a thumbs up... There are a number of emojis that are appropriate when sent in small doses. However, an entire firework display of hearts or unicorns doesn't quite befit a more technically oriented negotiation.

You have opened your negotiation and only a few partners have turned on their cameras. What can you do? You: "Hi, Tim, it's nice to see you. How's it going?" Small talk ... "Ah! Luis, you're with us, too. Do you also have a camera? It's better when we can see each other" ... Pause ... wait ... "Oh good, Luis, it seems it's working for you too. Hi, how are you ..."

VIRTUAL NEGOTIATION. BEST PRACTICE

At the very beginning, be sure to indicate that you would appreciate it if participants turned on their cameras, and kindly request everyone present to do so. At times, you may need to address individuals directly by name, and if necessary, follow up. Also, be prepared to endure the silence that may ensue. This initial investment is well worth it: The atmosphere of virtual negotiation is much more personal with cameras turned on. Even after breaks (during which you should turn off both your camera and your microphone to regain your focus in private), it may occasionally be necessary to mention this once again in a friendly manner.

VIRTUAL NEGOTIATION. TIP #14

Focus on you, the negotiator! Being in front of the camera

In video conferences, your background plays a significant role because, apart from you, the background is the only thing visible in the frame. Even from your home office, an insight into your private space come look professional.

Choosing the appropriate background

It is best to go with a subtle background. An extensive bookshelf is impressive, but unsettling. Your kitchen cabinet, with all of your herbs and spices, oil, and vinegar, may reveal that you like to cook, but is inappropriate for a serious negotiation. If you want to make an authentic and competent impression, your background should complement you visually rather than compete with you. If you don't work in the tourism industry, an exotic palm tree wallpaper is rather unsuitable, as it may lead your virtual negotiation partners more towards daydreaming than focused collaboration. The same goes for other vacation or leisure photos, no matter how big or small.

A blank white wall is not absolutely necessary to make a professional impression. On the contrary, a tidy and tasteful setup in the background can add spatial depth, as it provides your face with a stylish frame. Carefully consider the objects in the background so that they don't distract from you as a negotiator or cast an unfavorable light on you. By now, word has gotten around that a case of beer, your laundry basket, or your ironing board should be far away from view. Even though you may want to make the environment a little cozier with plants, the rule of thumb here is: less is more. Look at your thumbnail image and examine your face, remove any visual disruptions, or adjust your camera's position so that you remain optimally visible. Some office chairs with a very high backrest are reminiscent of a throne rising behind the negotiator. Gaming chairs that immediately reveal the gamer in you are just as unsuitable. If possible, position yourself so that your upper body is in front of a solid or calm background with spatial depth. If you have very little space, find the most visually quiet place in the background. Also, think about any family members who might walk through the frame during the video conference, perhaps to get to the refrigerator, and ask them to please stay away during your meeting. Clutter, such as an untidy desk in the background, also draws attention away from you as the negotiator. Ensure an undisturbed atmosphere.

If the space in your home office is limited, you can put up a partition wall or a screen. The advantage of these options over a virtual background is that you can design them. Even a bouquet of flowers in a beautiful vase, a few branches from the garden, or a special picture can add accents without being distracting. You can also drop a hint about one of your hobbies: With a bicycle in the background, you provide a conversation starter for small talk just like with a guitar hung on the wall.

The opportunities and risks of virtual backgrounds

Virtual backgrounds are widely used today and are considered professional. You didn't have time to tidy up the living room, or you had to temporarily relocate to your child's room for organizational reasons? Both the mess next to the couch and your daughter's pink wallpaper can be made invisible with just a few clicks. Dialing in from a hotel room? With a virtual background, the scene definitely appears more formal than an unmade hotel bed. Many companies also provide their employees with virtual backgrounds with the organization's logo, which is a beneficial way to convey a sense of cohesion. When negotiating virtually as a team from different locations, having a shared company background allows the opposite party's negotiators to instantly recognize you as representatives of your company. One disadvantage of virtual backgrounds, whether with a company logo or individually "blurred," is that negotiators are perceived as more impersonal and closed off. Allowing a glimpse into your own four walls is a leap of faith, while a virtual background deliberately and categorically excludes anything private. It's a bit like a negotiator in a face-to-face negotiation crossing their arms, leaning back, and watching you with a poker face, not revealing anything about themselves for now. From a technical standpoint, virtual backgrounds are a challenge to the performance of many computers. Often the contours are not separated sharply enough from the background. That's why when the person moves around, their hair, especially curls and fringed haircuts, appears visually distorted. Depending on the colors and the way the light is shining, even some elements of your living spaces will flash through from time to time. This can sometimes result in ghostly-looking negotiation partners. It's amusing, but not really beneficial or business-like.

VIRTUAL NEGOTIATION. BEST PRACTICE

In summary, it's advisable to minimize visual and auditory distractions. Allow visual calm to set in. Don't use a virtual background; instead, arrange a space in your home office that presents you in a **professional,** appealing, and natural manner.

VIRTUAL NEGOTIATION. TIP #15

Spot on! The right light

Even in front of the screen, negotiators want to appear in the right light. However, the reality sometimes looks different. Does this sound familiar? The people you are supposed to be negotiating with appear as very dark, barely discernible, or ghostly pale figures. It's unsightly and distracts from the actual negotiation. How can virtual negotiators optimally illuminate their faces? In general, it's important to ensure that light does not shine on the camera from behind. This happens if you sit with your back to a source of light. You will then only be perceived as a dark shadow. Your facial expressions will no longer be perceived by the negotiating party. Avoid backlighting by closing curtains or blinds or turning off lights from behind. It's better to go with frontlighting, which involves positioning your desk in a way that the light either comes directly from the front or perhaps from the front but off to the side a bit. In bright rooms, you usually don't need another source of light. If you are sitting directly in front of a window or if a spotlight is shining directly on your face, you may find yourself squinting to protect your eyes from the brightness, resulting in a grim facial expression. For extended periods of times, the alternation between bright sunlight and the screen is very tiring for your eyes. If working from your company's offices, be sure to reserve a bright meeting room well in advance. If you don't have enough natural light, get a ring light or softbox. Both are affordable and can be purchased for as little as 25 euros.

Using ring lights for precise illumination

Ring lights are best positioned at eye level to the right or left of the monitor, preferably on height- and angle-adjustable stands. It is worth investing in slightly higher quality ring lights that let you control the brightness with a dimmer. This allows you to adjust the desired brightness to the time of day.

Softboxes for people with glasses

Professional photographers use softboxes for harmonious, soft, and evenly diffused light. With a softbox you can control the illumination of the desired subject and keep any unwanted shadows to a minimum. Softboxes are particularly suitable for people who wear glasses, because if ring lights are used, a brightly illuminated circle can often be seen on the lenses of their glasses. This disturbs the people they are speaking with and reduces the perception of eye contact.

The appropriate light intensity

Photographers recommend a light intensity that corresponds to the sun on an overcast day. In other words, the goal of illumination from in front of a webcam is to have soft light coming from slightly above. Among the professionals it is no secret that the most beautiful portraits are taken in this light and not, as is commonly assumed, in bright sunshine. Soft light can be replicated at your desk with the proper lighting equipment. Bright artificial light or glaring sunlight that is too close to the subject causes the contours of the face to disappear during virtual negotiations (overexposure). Extremely bright light is also accompanied by harsh shadows that reveal the smallest imperfections of the skin, mercilessly spotlight every wrinkle and pimple, and make people's eyes disappear into dark caverns, all of which do not serve negotiators. If it's too dark – or the only source of light is behind you – your facial expressions will no longer be discernible. In fact, you may as well leave the camera turned off altogether. The optimal illumination of your face throughout virtual negotiations takes some time in advance to test out. Schedule a meeting with a friend or colleague, or set up a meeting with yourself so that you can try things out until you're happy with the results.

And here's what you need to do: For the best results, and if your particular location allows, position yourself facing a window that you can darken if it's sunny outside. Test this out during different times of day and in various weather conditions, as lighting conditions fluctuate between between dusk and dawn. When it gets dark, do you have ample sources of light around you that you can quickly turn on? It's possible that you will negotiate with partners from different time zones. How will you come across in the dark? How do lighting conditions change when the sun is shining, when the sky is overcast, or on a gray rainy day? What is the path of the sun, and at what time does the sun rise and set?

VIRTUAL NEGOTIATION. BEST PRACTICE

Ensure that there are sufficient sources of light in dark rooms. Turn on the ceiling lamp and an additional desk lamp in front of you. Check the illumination of your face every now and then during the day and make any necessary adjustments. Gradually adjust the brightness to a level that makes you look favorable.

Cold light is better than warm light

Also pay attention to the temperature of the light. What do I mean by that? Sources of light typically come in two different light temperatures: white and yellow. White is designed to mimic daylight and tends to be cooler and harsher. Yellowish light gives off a warm and cozy feel. What is the light temperature of the light sources you use? Do they resemble daylight or is the light very warm? In online negotiations, cold light is preferred over warm because it looks more natural and professional. Negotiators also come across as fresher and healthier. Furthermore, the source of light creates a slight sparkle in one's eyes, making one's gaze seem more vivid.

VIRTUAL NEGOTIATION. BEST PRACTICE

It's best to turn on your artificial light sources from the beginning, especially when your virtual negotiation is to start in daylight and continue into the darker hours of the day. This way, the transition from daylight to darkness is smooth, and you don't have to worry about your lighting anymore. You will be well illuminated throughout.

VIRTUAL NEGOTIATION. TIP #16

Boost your online impact through good virtual body language

Let's assume for a moment that all virtual negotiators have their cameras turned on. Everyone is clearly visible, awake, and present, and the technology is functioning properly. Now the bodies start talking through the computer screens. We impact others through our own body language, and conversely, others impact us through their non-verbal communication as well. In this negotiation tip, we will explore how to find the optimal framing and thus make the best use of the available space – our thumbnail. To make a good impression online, there are many factors to consider: the appropriate clothing, the most optimal styling, expressive makeup, and jewelry for women, and yes, even for men. Special advice will also be given to people who wear glasses. Even more than in face-to-face negotiations, our body language is mostly unconscious, as we are concentrated on many other things. Nevertheless, we do notice a few things online: first and foremost, the facial expressions of the other negotiating parties. Online, eye contact holds special significance, and it's not as easy as it may seem to maintain. Only when we can accurately interpret the gazes being sent through the ether and understand the significant impact of small hand gestures will we succeed in deciphering body language effectively in others and utilizing it ourselves in a virtual setting. One difficulty with speaking online is no longer being able to really look each other in the eye. We are essentially always looking underneath the person's eyes. Otherwise we would have to look directly into the camera to simulate normal eye contact, but we would then lose sight of the person's image. It's a real dilemma.

Do you know your optimal angle to the camera?

This will determine whether you'll be looking down on your negotiation partners, and they'll see more of your nostrils than your eyes, which can happen when your laptop has a built-in camera near the keyboard. It will also determine whether only your nose will be peeking out from the lower part of the screen, with sometimes more of your home office ceiling being visible than you yourself. Both scenarios are sub-optimal. Strive for eye-to-eye communication in virtual negotiations as well.

To do so, position the camera at the appropriate angle: Ideally, it should be at a right angle to your eyes. This may require you to place your laptop on a stack of books or a cardboard box. Certainly, you can find something useful in your home office. These days, it's not hard to find height-adjustable laptop stands. You can also connect an external keyboard and mouse to the laptop, this will give you a more comfortable typing position, should the laptop be too high.

Centered and at eye level – The optimal framing

If you are too close to the camera, your face will fill the entire screen and the negotiating parties will feel overwhelmed by your presence. If the distance between you and the camera is too great and you're too far away, you'll diminish your presence until you seem to blend in with the background. Recall the work of a professional photographer: Balanced business portraits have the eyes aligned with the upper third line. Apply this knowledge to your position in front of the camera and always face the screen head-on. As a guideline, your crown should be at the top end of the screen with some space to spare towards the edge. Your upper body should be visible up to the middle of your upper arm, but at most up to your elbow. If you are using a second screen, be sure to verify which camera is transmitting your image. Ensure that the person you are talking to sees you from the screen from which you have optimally aligned your camera.

VIRTUAL NEGOTIATION. BEST PRACTICE

Anyone who wears glasses is familiar with the problem of smudged and dirty lenses. Most of the time we're left wondering where these oil smudges and fingerprints have come from again. We often don't even realize how frequently we readjust our glasses after furrowing our brows or running our hands through our hair. Online, the smudges on our glasses become magnified and can be especially noticeable at high camera resolutions. Therefore, be sure to regularly clean your glasses.

Dress for online success

Each of us has our own taste when it comes to clothing. Every negotiator has their own style and personal preferences. We have always adapted to our position, the hierarchy, the industry, and the corporate culture. We have also dressed appropriately for face-to-face negotiations, which is something that we can continue to do. But the question of what kind of clothing supports one's impact on camera is one that many virtual negotiators ask themselves. Especially because only a small portion of us can be seen, the desire exists for it to be perfectly presented. Even if sweatpants are more comfortable to wear while we're in our home offices and no one sees them, we still project what we wear. Seemingly small details can have a significant impact, one that is often even more pronounced on screen than in regular business situations: An unironed shirt, a popped collar, or a worn-out sweater can also diminish your desired professional impact. If you are wearing a blazer, a jacket, or a sports coat with a collar, it may slide up and create an unsightly crease around the neck. Or the shoulder part has shifted to the left or right, making you appear crooked. To avoid this, smooth out the top and sit on your jacket if it's long enough.

VIRTUAL NEGOTIATION. BEST PRACTICE

Choose solid colored tops that convey a sense of calm. Narrow stripes, small checks, and finely patterned fabrics like pepita, glen check, or herringbone create the so-called moiré effect. This is an optical distortion that irritates the eye with an illusion of wavy shimmering movements and can be very distracting. Large patterns divert attention from your face by visually overpowering you.

Also, avoid bulky scarves that visually shorten your neck and steal the spotlight from you. If you are a woman, pay attention to the neckline of your top, which should still be visible within our online thumbnail, otherwise it will create the impression that you are showing a great deal of cleavage. Also, pay attention to your choice of color. Black and white are tricky colors because cameras intensify contrasts, which can lead to contours blurring within the clothing. In a black blouse, you'll look like a gloomy, disgruntled blob of color if the lighting is off. White clothing, in the worst-case scenario against a white background, can create a similar contourless effect, practically making you vanish. When you're in front of a computer screen, your choice in color can be a bit stronger than normal, because the screen swallows color. Especially in artificial light, your camera displays colors darker than they really are; dark blue and dark brown can quickly turn into black. A colorful piece of clothing makes an outfit come alive and can bring energy and freshness to your image by playing with contrasts. Shiny fabrics like satin silk, as well as decorative rhinestone elements, can lead to unattractive reflections under unfavorable lighting conditions. It's best to try out your clothing beforehand, especially with regard to the background.

Styling – Hair, make-up, and jewelry

The reduced cropping of the image that you are using to make an impact, the topic of hair and makeup is important. When we negotiate virtually, we may start to sweat. Make sure that your skin is not shiny. With a colorless, mattifying powder, men can also make areas such as the forehead, nose, chin, and any receding hairline less shiny on camera. Women can finally put on a bit more makeup. Since the camera swallows light, you often look paler online than you are in real life. As a rule of thumb – this also applies to television appearances or video recordings – about 30 percent more makeup can be used. Be careful with hair gel and hairspray. Any shine can make freshly washed and styled hair look greasy. Subtle jewelry is less distracting than jewelry that is too flashy. Wearing large earrings, especially, can cause unnecessary noise when wearing headsets. The same goes for big watches and bracelets that clank and rattle while you type.

VIRTUAL NEGOTIATION. BEST PRACTICE

Turn on your camera before going online. This will give you enough time to check and adjust the framing, background, and lighting. If your negotiating parties have already joined the meeting, it's too late.

Body language usually takes place subconsciously[15]

Take the opportunity to pay attention to how often you move without it being consciously directed. When you negotiate, you want to elicit a reaction from your counterpart through the impact of your words and body language. Consequently, the worst thing that could happen to you as a negotiator would be *not* to make an impact. So that you can consciously control your impact in the future and better read the messages that negotiating parties are sending you, in the following, you will learn some of the most important vocabulary for negotiation body language. Even if we can't see the other person's entire body and the image is only two-dimensional instead of three-dimensional, we are still able to perceive a lot online: the tension in a person's body and the position of their head, neck, and throat, the facial expressions with eye contact, nose, and mouth, shoulders, and sometimes arms and hands.

VIRTUAL NEGOTIATION. BEST PRACTICE

Your outer world reflects your inner one. Make sure you maintain an upright, activated posture even in front of the camera. This conveys presence. Make sure that you are sitting comfortably; otherwise, during the course of the virtual negotiation, you may start fidgeting around or gradually slump down like a deflating balloon. This will cause you to lose both inner and outer persuasiveness, which is crucial during negotiations. Sit up straight and avoid leaning against the backrest of your chair during critical moments.

Negotiators first perceive our facial expression

In most cases, the other person perceives our entire facial expression and not a particular detail. And our body follows the mind, our thoughts control our movements. We have more than 650 muscles, with over 50 in the face alone. Smiling requires 17 muscles, while frowning uses over 40. What fundamental signals does facial expression convey? When the overall movement is upward, like with a smile, a positive impact is achieved. When the overall movement is downward, however, we suspect fatigue, tension, or problems. But we have also learned that negotiators who want to deceive us first attempt to do so through their facial expressions. We quickly recognize a false smile, feigned friendliness, or a controlled poker face. At times, we perceive such signals as contradictions to other parts of the body. The credibility of negotiation partners can suffer as a result.

An interesting offer comes across as less attractive without eye contact

Look at the other party when you negotiate! Is your counterpart meeting your gaze? Is their gaze exuding confidence? Or is it demanding, probing, and dominant? No matter how the eye contact appears, you will receive feedback about your counterpart as a person and can discern whether their offer is sincere. Her are some recommendations on how to achieve a positive impact yourself:

- Eye contact for at least one second per person, for a maximum of three seconds per person
  A shorter duration is not perceived as eye contact. Recommendation for less experienced negotiators: Select one or two people in

front of you whom you find charismatic and look at them more often. Eye contact longer than three seconds comes across as staring.

- Intense eye contact when making demands
  You come across as resolute and lend weight to your demands if you combine them with intense eye contact. Do not look down when making or rejecting demands.

- Avoid a cold, calculating gaze.
  Don't forget the recommendation "Be gentle with the individual and firm on the issue!" Build a human connection through warm eye contact. If you fixate on your counterpart, they will inevitably feel uncomfortable. You won't build in trust this way.

- Lackluster gazes never stimulate anyone.
  The best arguments are useless if your eyes do not promise an experience.

- Engage negotiating parties with eye contact.
  Don't just look at the decision-maker from the other party, but make eye contact with everyone. Don't forget to involve the members of your own team as well.

- Every negotiation begins and ends with a short pause for a "look me in the eye!"
  At the beginning of the negotiation, before you even say anything, take a conscious look at the virtual negotiation participants. Give yourself and the other party time to concentrate with this initial eye contact. Eye contact will then remain more constant afterwards. And even if you've said the final word clearly and audibly, send another brief glance afterward.

What does it actually mean to look another person in the eye?

By looking someone in the eye, you build a connection and force the negotiating party to respond. We like to escape this compulsion with a little blink, a long bat of the eyelid. Simply looking to the side is often enough to avoid direct confrontation. Whenever the other person doesn't want to be forced into a decision, they will look the other way, so there's no need to explain it in words. In future negotiations, keep in mind that the other party may want to avoid making a definite statement if they are looking the other way. Take note of this, address it, or take a break to consider the next steps. You can also consciously make it easier for others by looking to the side yourself. Your counterpart will then be more relaxed during the negotiation and have time to reconsider their decision.

No walk in the park – How to maintain eye contact online

What applies to face-to-face negotiations also applies online: Looking into the eyes of the person you are talking to builds trust. Trust is important for developing good relationships in negotiations and achieving the best possible results. Online we also see ourselves, which is something unusual. We are always a little fascinated by ourselves, and it's not easy not to look at ourselves. An initial tip: Switch to the gallery view to reduce your image to a collective thumbnail size for all participants in the negotiation. If your software allows you to, you can also position the gallery view at the top of the screen. This way, you will intuitively look more often at the top of the screen, i.e. where the camera is usually located and where direct eye contact will be simulated. If you want to be even more professional, you can also work with eye tracking software. Eye tracking is a technology that is used to determine where a person is looking on the screen and can also help to establish eye contact. Microsoft Teams, for example, offers the "EyeContact" feature in its settings, which uses artificial intelligence (AI) to guide your gaze during virtual meetings. As the development of new technologies is rapid, it is best to research the latest state of the art. Regardless of whether the platform you use offers an eye tracking feature or you prefer to use stand-alone software: It is important to note that special hardware such as an eye-tracking camera may be required. For example, the start-up 4Tiitoo[16] from Munich offers NUIA Full Focus, a smart, gaze-controlled solution for establishing and maintaining eye contact with negotiating parties in video conferences. However, there are opposing opinions regarding the use of eye-tracking software, such as from TechCrunch, which advises against it to avoid the risk of appearing more like a robot and less like a human. It's best to try it out for yourself.

VIRTUAL NEGOTIATION. QR

The company IMOTIONS compared 10 different providers of eye tracking software. Here you can learn more.

Techcrunch advises against the use of eye tracking software in this article.

VIRTUAL NEGOTIATION. BEST PRACTICE

Look into the camera as often as possible when speaking. You can use the illuminated dot, which is usually located above or below the screen, as a guide if you are not using an external camera. This feels very unusual because you don't receive any response from the negotiating participants in real time. If you look at the thumbnails of the people with whom you are speaking, they will see you looking down, which comes across as less confident. Look the other person straight in the eye by looking directly into the camera, even if it doesn't feel like that's what you're doing. Stick a small post-it or a colored sticker next to the camera as a reminder.

Pay close attention to what else negotiators are expressing through their body language

Negotiators always express their degree of affectedness with their entire body. What of this can we observe in a virtual negotiation? It's the movement of the eyebrows, the wrinkling of the nose, earlobes, movements of the mouth, tension in the throat, neck, and shoulders, as well as gesticulating hands that give us a lot of indirect information.

What do negotiators express with their eyebrows?

Two raised eyebrows are a sign of maximum attention: Negotiators are demonstrating their effort to absorb as much information as possible with this gesture. In contrast, only one raised eyebrow signifies skepticism. The negotiator believes they are only getting half the truth.

Why do people often touch their glasses or earlobes?

The message is clear: Anyone who has discovered weaknesses in their own concept needs to take a closer look at it. Sometimes it's also the worry of having forgotten a detail. Surprisingly, negotiators who are insecure often grab their earlobes as if to stimulate their eyesight. In acupuncture, the stimulation point for better vision is in fact located on the earlobe. Sometimes, however, it is just a gesture of embarrassment, a signal of physicality in the face of the virtual thumbnail. So, the question arises: Where should you put your hands when you're not taking notes? Because they are looking for a place to go, they quickly end up near the earlobes. So, be attentive and don't overinterpret signals!

What is the significance of the mouth when it comes to body language?

We allow things to enter our bodies through our mouths. It conveys an immediate and intuitive message about what's good for us with a smile, and what's harmful through downturned corners of the mouth. In this sense, the mouth is a direct mirror of the negotiating party's state of mind.

And what do the lips have to say?

A pursed mouth indicates a refusal to take anything in. In negotiation, this signals resistance to new ideas or approaches from the other party. In contrast, relaxed lips indicate an open mind.

What does it mean when negotiators touch their noses?

The nose is one of the final points of judgment. In a figurative sense, we are assessing what seems palatable and what doesn't. If someone in a negotiation quotes a price and touches their nose, they fear their offer may be too high. Seen in this light, holding your nose is a sign of critical examination and thoughtfulness. Or a person may just have an itchy nose.

A smile before you say anything works wonders!

We can only temporarily control our facial expressions. However, it is unnecessary to keep them under control all the time anyway. Most people are reluctant to practice a certain facial expression just to increase their impact. We want to make a contribution to negotiations, we want to inform or convince – not act! Nevertheless, we don't like stiff facial expressions. We can easily do something to come across as friendly. Look at the participants openly and sympathetically. Neutral topics can also use a friendly face. A smile always reflects positive charisma. If possible, avoid the following patterns:

- **Embarrassed laughter**
  The eyes of the timid negotiator appear questioning, the smile never seems quite complete.

- **Laughing at someone**
  Ironic laughter changes the area around the eyes. The eyes narrow slightly, sometimes with one eyebrow raised.

- **Fake laughter**
  A simulated laugh does not come across as authentic. A person often shows their teeth, while their expression seems frozen.

- **Cold laughter**
  Cold laughter occurs when the eyes do not laugh. Most of the time, the head remains upright, and the gaze fixates on the other party. The laughter seems to be a preview of personal triumph.

What significance does the neck have for negotiators?

The neck allows the head to move, providing a view of things. Negotiators with a flexible neck are open all around. They not only see the familiar, but also the new and unknown. What kinds of neck postures can we observe in negotiations? The upright, straight, almost stiff posture of the neck signals "I stand by what I say." People "at attention" clearly stick to their goals. What lies to the left and right of the path is seen as a distraction. In many cultures, this attitude is appreciated for the reliability it indicates, even if critics may call it narrow-minded. For negotiators with this underlying attitude, avoiding, giving in, and compromising are seen as negative. If your opponent's neck stiffens in the middle of the negotiation, you can be sure that you have just hit a weak point in your argument. If their tension eases, and their head tilts, you have won the other person over. What signals does a head tilted slightly to the side send to the negotiating party? It signals your willingness to explore alternative paths. You are avoiding direct confrontation. Negotiators also express understanding by tilting their heads. It is often easier for negotiating parties to admit mistakes or problems when they see their counterpart's head tilted.

When negotiators put their hand on their throat, it means that they are trying to cover up a weakness. Perhaps your counterpart does not know what is expected or how an argument can be formulated.

Internal energy reserves for negotiation

The heart and lungs, our body's own energy reserves, are located in the chest and you should make the best possible use of them during the negotiation. When you breathe deeply, your lungs are filled with oxygen. This also increases your energy levels and intensifies your radiance of vitality. The sound of your voice becomes richer, and your shoulders and shoulder blades become looser. This relaxed posture allows your breathing to flow freely and creates mobility and the ability to take action. Shallow breathing, on the other hand, makes you feel insecure and reduces your ability to maintain an activated posture. The result is a negative impression resulting from your sunken chest. A lack of oxygen is also evident in the fact that your voice no longer carries and appears unsteady.

When do negotiators hold their breath?

Anything that makes you doubt or confronts you with a decision during a negotiation makes you hold your breath. Negotiators who breathe in and out evenly as proposals are made to them are usually not surprised by this. If negotiators briefly hold their breath, this means that they are thinking about an offer. They are taking a moment to be still. The decision is made at this very moment: Will I accept the offer or reject it?

When the weight of the world is on your shoulders

Straight shoulders signalize: I am not carrying any weight, neither physically nor mentally. Anything that burdens a negotiator weighs down on their shoulders and curves their back. In the face of danger, we instinctively pull our heads in and raise our shoulders. In today's negotiations, we no longer carry literal weight, rather our weight is responsibility. You have probably heard the following comments in negotiations: "I am responsible for" or "I have the responsibility to." If you suffer under the burden of responsibility, your flexibility will be limited. What are negotiators expressing when they give you the cold shoulder instead of the center of their body? Rejection. The cold shoulder is also always an inflexible shoulder. The attached arm remains lifeless and can neither give nor take. Someone who negotiates over the cold shoulder talks as if they were speaking to a wall. Flexibility will be impossible in such a negotiation.

The pointing finger and the porcupine: understanding gesturing

What does it mean if your supervisor keeps "stabbing" you with his pen? Why are the new employee's knuckles turning white as chalk while he is proposing his new concept? Why does the sales colleague always lose control of her hands when it's her turn? Online negotiation seems to be a true opera stage, a place of major gestures and minor awkwardness. But what's behind all these movements? With the consciously or unconsciously used guidance of their arms and hands, the negotiator supports their spoken words. At the same time, gesturing always reflects one's inner state. Generally, a negotiator comes across as open when their arms and hands appear free enough to move away from their body, neither closing them off nor making them seem stiff. One's own gestures are natural when they do not come from the wrist, but from the elbow, or even from the shoulder in people with strong motor skills. Especially online, fast gestures appear jerky and hectic, while slow gestures convey a calmer and more controlled impression. The extended finger is referred to as the "pistol" and is a dominant gesture, while praying hands with raised fingers are defensive and especially observed in negotiators who feel cornered, which is why this gesture is also called the "porcupine." The quills are thrown for their own protection.

The three basic hand movements: open, concealed, and dominant

Every negotiator uses all three basic forms of hand movements. Depending on their character, they may use some more than others.

- **The concealed hand movement**
  Those who only show the back of their hand to their counterpart during negotiations are hiding the sensitive palm of their hand. Negotiating parties are given the feeling that the other person has something to hide.

- **The open hand movement**
  In contrast, with the open movement, negotiators show their palms and signal: I am revealing what I have in my hands, and in doing so I am revealing that I have nothing to hide. They are not afraid that someone might take something away from them, but seem willing to share with others and agree to compromise in negotiation. Open hands naturally tend to move upward; their natural movements extend outward and upward. We associate

such a radius with generosity and self-assuredness. Giving with an open hand means not forcing anything on the other person. Such an offer is presented as if on a tray. Negotiators may decide for themselves whether or not to accept the offer. Whenever you make open offers, make sure that your hand remains in the open gesture for at least two seconds so that your counterpart has enough time to reach out. Imagine someone offering you a piece of cake on a tray and immediately withdrawing the tray. They would think the offer was not meant seriously. The fast movement contains a hint of aggression. Behind this is the fear of being rejected. However, if you stand behind your offer, you need not fear rejection. An additional advantage of the open hand is that it prevents the dominant pointing finger effect and you avoid patronizing the other party. The more open gestures you get into the habit of making, the more positive your impact will be.

■ **The dominant hand movement**

Dominant hand movements exert pressure. They move from top to bottom. This pushing down has a suppressive effect. In a dominant gesture lies the desire to assert oneself over another person, if necessary, against their will. Dominant negotiators rarely have a positive impact because of this behavior.

VIRTUAL NEGOTIATION. KNOWLEDGE

Status elevators and status reducers in virtual body language

When negotiators come together, body language often sends unconscious signals as to who is higher in the pecking order. This unconscious clarification of status also takes place in virtual negotiations. However, the reduced perception of others' body language often makes it more difficult to decipher. In an online meeting, the CEO has the same thumbnail size as the experts supporting them;

their body signals cannot be immediately deciphered in a compact 3D view. Power is demonstrated in body language through status elevating signals. Virtual negotiators can observe subordination through status-reducing aspects.

	High status	Low status
Eye contact	▪ Maintaining intensive eye contact from a confrontational posture ▪ Very little blinking ▪ Eye contact is perceived as pleasant up to approx. three seconds, but if it lasts longer, it becomes increasingly unpleasant. Staring can also happen online!	▪ Brief, nervous eye contact ▪ Breaking eye contact and then quickly glancing back ▪ Looking down with one's head tilted to the side
Taking up space and gesturing	▪ Taking up space where several screens are present ▪ Faster access to information possible ▪ Most of the space is taken up either by speech or silence ▪ Big sweeping gestures	▪ Small-scale and erratic gestures ▪ Self-soothing gestures ▪ Information is laboriously searched for in files
Sternum and shoulders	▪ Showing the "hero's chest" – pushing the chest forward ▪ Almost creating a hollow back ▪ Shoulders hunched down and back	▪ Showing the "chicken chest" – pushing one's chest backwards ▪ Rounding the back ▪ Sunken shoulders

Head posture and head movements	■ Head kept straight ■ Chin raised upwards ■ Slow head movements	■ Head tilted to the side ■ Restless and nervous head movements ■ Leaning on one's chin during a conversation
Facial expressions and smiling	■ Little to no smile emphasizes seriousness ■ All the way to a poker face, so as not to reveal internal processes to the outside world	■ Lots of smiling, often in combination with frequent nodding ■ Even to the point of smiling in embarrassment to make unpleasant situations less tense
Body activation	■ Body is highly activated ■ All the way to excessive tension, which can have an aggressive impact on others	■ Little or even no body activation ■ Quick and non-activated gesturing

VIRTUAL NEGOTIATION. BEST PRACTICE

Don't move around too much in front of the screen: Big gestures and constantly shifting back and forth tend to be confusing and can lead to disruptions in the transmission of your video. Print out all the information in advance so that you don't have to look for anything during the negotiation. You should also refrain from drinking coffee or eating snacks while the camera is turned on. Cookies, potato chips, and their packaging can make really loud rustling noises. If you have a drink next to you, make sure that the cup or glass is clean and not covered in droplets or limescale. The wide-angle lenses of the cameras will magnify these as if with a magnifying glass every time you take a sip.

The range of movement of your upper body depends on your sitting position

If you position your feet too far forward, your upper body will automatically lean backwards. You cannot show your appreciation for the other negotiators in this way. If your legs are straight or slightly back, it will be easier for you to lean towards the others.

Negotiators who lean to the side during a conversation are evasive – either rationally or emotionally. They remain receptive, but avoid taking a clear stance themselves. From negotiation partners who lean to the side, you will hear responses such as: "I still need to think about that" or "Interesting, we should discuss that point again later." Try to straighten up "wobbly" negotiating parties. Only from such a posture will they be able to make clear, precise statements.

VIRTUAL NEGOTIATION. BEST PRACTICE

Try out two variations at home in front of your webcam: 1. Three-minute news broadcast variation: Speak like a news anchor, using very few gestures. 2. Present for three minutes with calm and deliberate gesturing. Record both variations and watch the results. Which do you like better? With which do you feel more comfortable? Which kind of impact appeals to you more? You can also ask a colleague or friend to give you feedback or join you for a practice meeting.

WOLFGANG SCHATZ

Wolfgang Schatz is an actor. He has had roles in *Tatort*, *Die Rosenheim Cops*, *Der Bulle von Tölz*, *Derrick*, and many other productions. He also works as a voice actor for *The Simpsons* and *South Park*. Wolfgang Schatz has worked as a seminar actor and project manager since 2007. He led the Global Siemens Negotiation Excellence Training with more than 1,200 participants in 18 countries.

J.P. Wolfgang, how does virtual negotiation change our perception of body language?

W.S. I see two main aspects to this: When people negotiate virtually without consciously thinking about it, they tend to only passively interpret the body language of their negotiation partner and may not feel the need to be proactive in their own body language. For example, just using a virtual background on platforms like Zoom and Teams often leads people to stay still and not move around much. However, those who actively and consciously approach virtual negotiation can gain real advantages in the outcomes of their negotiations.

J.P. What tips do you have for online negotiation from an actor's perspective?

W.S. A technically professional appearance significantly increases your external impact. The setting, lighting, camera, sound, and stability of the connection should be perfect. The height of the camera lens – preferably an external one – should be at the same height as your eyes. This enables negotiators to "meet at eye level" in the truest sense of the expression. This is one of the fundamental prerequisites for cooperative negotiation. During key parts of the negotiation, negotiators should ideally look directly into the camera – in other words, not down, where they can see the other party on the monitor. This makes the negotiating party feel that they are being addressed directly. Negotiators can make online presentations more effective and interesting by interrupting the presentation mode after every four to six slides and displaying an enlarged view of themselves for an example or anecdote that relates to the topic.

J.P. To respond in a differentiated, direct, and quick manner to the type of person you are dealing with, you recommend using the DISC personality model, which is based on the individual classification into the four basic types of dominance, influence, steadiness, and conscientiousness. How does this work? And what do you recommend for dealing with negotiators who can be classified under four personality types?

W.S. I would be happy to give you a few tips on how to deal with the four types. Dominant negotiators expect brief small talk. For example, the negotiating parties can ask how much time is available right at the beginning of the conversation. My tip: Always use clear, precise hand movements to emphasize your negotiating position, meaning avoid deliberately waving your hands around. Move a little closer to the camera so that you appear taller and stronger if necessary. If you think the other party's demands are excessive, react immediately, e.g. by shaking your head or saying a clear "no." Competitive negotiators sometimes provoke by turning off their camera in the middle of the negotiation. If the other party has not turned on the camera at the beginning, ask for clarification and request that it be turned on. If the other party refuses, then you should also turn your camera off.

J.P. Influence personality types are considered optimistic and open-minded. What is the best way for virtual negotiators to deal with them?

W.S. Influence negotiators love extensive small talk, as everything is linked to emotions. One trick is to position a personal item visibly behind you. This could be an item related to your hobby, a picture, a musical instrument, or sports equipment that appears to be casually leaning against the wall – and immediately invites the other person to ask interested questions. This also gives you a topic that you can pick up on again later. Active body language immediately brings people closer together and anything can be linked to emotions: "I'm glad," "What a shame …," "That irritates me …." To influence personality types, the relationship to their counterpart can be more important than the outcome of the negotiation. This knowledge could also be used as leverage virtually. As soon as an I-type strays away from your intended goal, you can show your disappointment non-verbally by shaking your head or giving a seemingly unconscious sigh. An I-type will now try to give in.

J.P. Then there are the negotiators in the DISC model who are predominantly calm and relaxed: those with the steadiness personality type. What advice would you give negotiators for the steadiness types?

W.S. If you see them with a steaming cup of coffee or tea, you will immediately feel more relaxed. You can also carry this mood over to your negotiation later on. There are no surprises; everything is transparent. Position yourself with your camera in front of a wall of books or in a cozy seating area. Proceed step by step and avoid exaggerated starting positions or making big gestures. Announce any major changes in advance so that your counterpart is not surprised.

J.P. Is it true that the conscientious personality types prefer not to switch on their camera? What can negotiators do about this?

W.S. Yes, conscientious people feel more at ease this way and are more in their comfort zone. Nevertheless, it is helpful for them to see the person they are talking to. It's best to send the note "Please turn on your camera for our call" with the Zoom or Teams invitation. Send out your agenda in advance so that you have a clear structure for entering the world of C-types. Avoid active body language and gesturing. Your voice should be calm and matter-of-fact throughout. The person you are talking to will probably answer your initial question "How are you?" with a simple "Good" – and thus signal that you should get straight to the point. At this point, however, switch to business small talk and show genuine interest by asking questions, e.g. about the other person's current project. Then even someone who is more matter-of-fact or detail-oriented will be prepared to open up. Avoid rhetorical softeners such as "of course," "somehow," "simply," or "I have to say," as this would reveal you as superficial in the eyes of a C-type. Support each argument in detail with objective criteria and comprehensible arguments.

VIRTUAL NEGOTIATION. QR

Here you can learn more about Wolfgang Schatz.

Here you can learn more about the DISC personality model.

VIRTUAL NEGOTIATION. TIP #17

The tone sets the tune: Your voice on the microphone

"In the right key one can say anything. In the wrong key, nothing: The only delicate part is the establishment of the key." This sentence by Bernhard Shaw applies to negotiations, especially. Your voice goes straight, without filters, and instantly into the hearts of the other negotiators, opening them to the message behind your words. Your voice can identify you as credible, determined, likable, and competent more than anything else in your appearance – or, conversely, it can fail to do so. Your voice is significantly responsible for revealing your inner emotions. Your tone shows whether you stand by your words or whether doubts, uncertainty, boredom, or displeasure are preoccupying you. Your voice and manner of speaking are indicators of your authenticity. The technical transmission and the microphone pose additional challenges for negotiators online.

Every voice is unique, as unmistakable as a fingerprint

Voice coach Eva Loschky[17] reports on an experiment conducted by the Max Planck Institute in Leipzig. Researchers there decoded the hidden messages in the sound of the voice. When we meet new negotiating parties, they immediately trigger a neurobiological resonance in us, whether we like it or not. Eye contact, voice, manner of speaking, facial expressions, and body movements evoke a spectrum of mirror reactions in us. Mirror neurons activate within us what were initially only the non-verbal signals of the negotiating party themselves. By sensing the feelings of another person within ourselves, we gain a spontaneous, intuitive understanding of what moves others. "What comes around goes around." What folk wisdom describes so simply, science explains as follows: Our brain stores these experiences with bodily states as so-called somatic markers. Either the non-verbal demeanor of the other negotiating party gives you confidence and inspires you, or their voice and demeanor come across as unfriendly and do not inspire confidence. These unconsciously triggered perceptions trigger bodily reactions in us. We also store these unconsciously in connection with the respective negotiating party. Whenever you think of this person later, you reactivate exactly these physical states. As a negotiator, you have already exerted influence within the first three seconds of a negotiation through your voice and your appearance, long before your counterpart recognizes and processes the meaning of your words. Various disciplines deal with the significance of experiential knowledge: decision theory, neurology, and psychology. You can think of your adaptive unconscious as a kind of supercomputer that rapidly and imperceptibly processes vast amounts of data that come your way.

VIRTUAL NEGOTIATION. BEST PRACTICE

Your voice plays a key role in virtual negotiations. It conveys appreciation, curiosity, compassion, warmth, and sympathy to the negotiating parties. It's more enjoyable to listen to a negotiator with a pleasant voice rather than one with an unpleasant voice. Fortunately, almost every healthy voice sounds good when used with the right speaking and sentence techniques.

Negotiation expert Chris Voss, who spent many years negotiating with hostage-takers for the FBI, writes in his book *Never Split the Difference: Negotiating As If Your Life Depended On It?*[18] about his experiences in extreme situations. In negotiations with dangerous hostage-takers, the aim is to prevent escalation, as this can cost lives. To stay in the conversation, Chris Voss has developed a "late-night FM DJ voice" over the years. He speaks like a radio DJ, presenting a deep, soft, slow, and confident voice late at night. Voss believes that negotiators can see their voice as a tool with which they can involuntarily achieve neurological telepathy. He even goes so far as to say that the voice is the most powerful instrument a negotiator has, that negotiators can use it to flip an emotional switch in the other party's brain. From mistrust to trust, from nervousness to calm. In addition to the voice of the late-night DJ, Voss uses two other voices: the positive, playful voice, with which he conveys confidence and optimism in the belief that goals can be achieved, and the firm, strong voice to put a stop to things and say no. For most of the time he spends negotiating,

Voss uses a playful, positive voice that represents an easygoing, light, and uplifting character. The key to using a positive, playful voice is to smile when we speak. The tonal effect also unconsciously influences the other party on the phone or in virtual negotiations without the use of a camera.

VIRTUAL NEGOTIATION. BEST PRACTICE

Speak even more clearly and distinctly online than in face-to-face negotiations. Modulate! Try out highs and lows. Speak in short, clear sentences, because then your voice will automatically return to the lower register. Such sentences are better received. Think of the late-night DJ.

VIRTUAL NEGOTIATION. BEST PRACTICE

The rule of thumb in online negotiations is: Speak in a way that is appropriate to the situation. Try to find common ground with the person you are talking to through your manner of speaking. The more formal and official a speaking and conversational situation is, or the more proper your counterpart speaks, the more you should adapt to this manner of speaking. The more relaxed, familiar, and informal an online negotiation is, the more likely you are to stick with colloquial language.

VIRTUAL NEGOTIATION. THINKING TIME

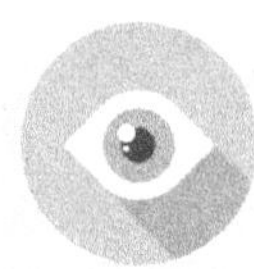

In Chapter 5, you learned about the limitations of body language in virtual negotiation and how you can increase your impact through your appearance in your thumbnail. I presented five valuable tips that will help you. Which one is your favorite that you will remember and use in your next online negotiation?

Tip #13: Don't speak into the void: Turn your camera on

....

Tip #14: Focus on you, the negotiator! Being in front of the camera

....

Tip #15: Spot on! The right light

....

Tip #16: Boost your online impact through good virtual body language

....

Tip #17: The tone sets the tune: Your voice on the microphone

....

CHAPTER 6. Yes, It's Possible!

Exerting Influence in Virtual Negotiations

The art of exerting influence is a key skill of successful negotiators, the superpower par excellence. In the following chapter, you will learn how you can harness this superpower in virtual negotiations. You will recognize why it is important to first have clarity about the primary goal and only then develop the appropriate strategy. A key decision for negotiators is whether they want to cooperate or compete with each other. If you are to collaborate on a long-term basis, you will strive for a mutually satisfactory result. Perhaps you are already familiar with the five principles of negotiation according to the Harvard Concept and are wondering how they can be applied online. If you are in competition with the other negotiating party and are interested in maximizing your own success, then you want to take the biggest piece of the pie possible. In competitive negotiation, classic negotiating tactics such as the rules of concession are used, or perhaps even your box of negotiating tricks is opened. But can the same tactics also be used virtually? You will discover what options you have and where the small and subtle differences lie in virtual negotiation. This chapter also explains what you can do if you encounter difficulties online and how you can stay in control despite the adversity.

Why people negotiate

People negotiate because better results can be achieved with negotiation than without it. This means that the result of the negotiation leads to added value. Sound abstract? It isn't at all. Good negotiators actively influence negotiations in order to achieve an outcome that is in their own favor. It is interesting to consider how the success of a virtual negotiation can be measured. When it comes to negotiation, there is essentially no one right solution, no one perfect result. It's a bit like beauty: Satisfaction is in the eye of the beholder.

What defines a good negotiation result

The quality of a negotiation can be measured by three different factors:

1. Its effectiveness: How satisfied are virtual negotiators with the quality of the actual result, i.e. what is written in the contracts at the end?
2. Its efficiency: How many resources, i.e. time and staff time, did the virtual negotiation take up?
3. The negotiation environment: What is the quality of the relationship between the negotiating parties? Has the relationship improved or gotten worse?

The assessment of satisfaction with a negotiation result is never completely objective. However, there is always a consensus on the following points: A good negotiation result is clear, i.e. unambiguous in its interpretation. It is achievable and therefore not a pipe dream. At the same time, it's fair, which means no one gets ripped off, and it benefits both sides. Last but not least, a good negotiation result is sustainable. It is supported by both sides and does not require renegotiation.

The two main styles of negotiation

Even in virtual negotiations, two different approaches can be adopted to deal with the other party: a cooperative approach, when you see the other person as a partner and want to achieve a mutually satisfactory result, and a competitive approach. This essentially involves asserting oneself against the other party. The other person is seen as an opponent and must be defeated. Let's compare the two basic approaches in more detail.

The competitive approach

We learn to make threats as early as in the sandbox: "If you don't give me your shovel, then you'll never be able to use my bucket again." Even four-year-olds emphasize their words through body language by taking a stance in front of their kindergarten friend. The underlying belief is that there can only be one winner, that the winner will be the person who asserts themselves, and that that person is me. The other person is going to lose. Learned early on, behavioral patterns develop quickly, which people continue to fine-tune throughout their lives in negotiation. The power of the strongest to get what they want then goes on and on. If the buyer says to the supplier "We have five competitors who are offering more favorable conditions," then the supplier starts to sweat and calculates in their head how much of a discount they can give.

Characteristics of the competitive negotiation style:

- The other party is my opponent, and opponents have to be defeated.
- The time orientation is designed for the short term, which means I have to win here and now. This is why the competitive style is more common in one-off negotiations.
- The negotiator tries to take the biggest possible slice of the pie.
- The negotiation process is marked by antagonism and the use of power and tricks.
- Personal effort is used to assert one's own interests, with no regard for the interests of others.
- The relationship is characterized by mistrust and suspicion, and sometimes the opponent becomes an enemy – and must be destroyed.

The cooperative approach

At the same time, we also learn from an early age that we belong to a social community and that we can only get along with others in the long term if we find common solutions. In kindergarten, we voluntarily share what's in our lunchbox because later on, during art time, we'll also share the crayons. Peaceful coexistence is based on giving and taking. We want not only ourselves, but also others and the community to be satisfied. This creates a sense of togetherness and solidarity. This also continues in our professional lives. During a price negotiation, you are more inclined to accommodate a supplier who won't let you down in emergency situations.

Characteristics of the cooperative negotiation style:

- The other party is a partner, and both sides should be satisfied with the result.
- The time orientation is designed for the long term, i.e. giving and taking alternate over a longer period of time.
- Negotiators try to enlarge the pie together and then distribute it fairly.
- The negotiation process is marked by creativity, flexibility, and joint problem solving.
- Personal effort is also invested in the service of others in order to find a mutually beneficial solution.
- The relationship is strengthened after the negotiation, trust is created, and both negotiating parties are put at ease. A spirit of mutual reliability develops as a basis for future cooperation.

VIRTUAL NEGOTIATION. BEST PRACTICE

The choice of negotiation style is not dependent on the choice of negotiation type. Both cooperative and competitive negotiations can be conducted virtually.

Develop the suitable dramaturgy

In theatre, dramaturgy refers to the study of the selection and arrangement of narrative devices. From the very beginning, dramaturges have the big picture of a stage play in mind. They plan the script based on this big picture. They sort and filter, compose, and develop individual scenes. They cast actors and support the director with strategies and ideas. In the film industry, a script doctor is also sometimes called upon to eliminate errors in the screenplay. At the end, the theatergoers sit in the foyer and enjoy the premiere. If you apply the idea of dramaturgy to negotiations, the following recommendations arise:

- Start designing the appropriate dramaturgy for your virtual negotiation at an early stage so that it becomes a great success.
- Make a clear decision in favor of cooperation, competition, or a combination of both negotiation styles.
- Familiarize yourself with proven negotiation techniques so that you can use the right tools and remain flexible.
- Familiarize yourself with the tactical tricks of both cooperative and competitive negotiation.
- Inquire in advance who the negotiating parties are so that you can assess the personalities of your counterparts even without having to first see them in person.
- Prepare for different scenarios and run through them with your team so that you are well prepared for potential pitfalls in remote negotiations.
- To prepare, use the following checklist, which is divided into a general and a personal section.

Checklist to prepare for virtual negotiations

■ **GENERAL PREPARATION**

Topic:

....

Participants:
- ■ Will you negotiate alone or in a team?
- ■ Who from your side will take part?
- ■ Who will take on which role in the team?
- ■ Who from the other party will take part?
- ■ Who will facilitate the negotiation?

Date and time:
- ■ Has the invitation/link been sent?
- ■ How long is the negotiation planned for?
- ■ Will there be a follow-up appointment? When can the follow-up appointment take place?
- ■ By when do you want to have achieved a result?

Language:

....

Materials:
- ■ Have documents been reviewed in preparation for the negotiation?
- ■ Have all parties received the relevant documents?

Organization:
- ■ Have all the technical requirements been met?
- ■ Which meeting software will you use to negotiate? Are you familiar with the most important functions?
- ■ Do you have a stable Internet connection?
- ■ Is an alternative communication channel necessary?

■ **PERSONAL PREPARATION**

1. What higher-level goals are you pursuing
   - with regards to the specific matter being negotiated?
   - with regards to any personal goals?
   - Are you negotiating as an agent (on behalf of) or principal (for your own purposes)?
   - Is there a hidden agenda?

2. What is your specific goal (ZOPA = Zone of Possible Agreement)?
   - What is your minimum goal (reservation point)?
   - What is your realistic goal?
   - What is your maximum goal?
   - What does your opening offer look like (anchor)?

3. How is the negotiating power distributed?
   - What is your BATNA (Best Alternative to Negotiated Agreement – Plan B)?
   - What is the (presumed) BATNA of the other party?

4. How well do you know the other party?
   - Do you have any previous experience with them? In person?
   - Are you meeting the other party virtually for the first time?
   - What can you learn in advance?

5. What are the interests of the other party?
   - Are there common interests?
   - What result will benefit both sides?
   - Where are the conflicts of interest?

6. How will you handle information?
   - What will you reveal to the other party?
   - What will you keep to yourself?
   - What information do you need from the other party?

7. What are just conjectures for now?
- What are your assumptions?
- What assumptions might the other party have about you?
- Do you want to dispel, accept, or reinforce these assumptions?

8. Are you negotiating just one point or an entire package of them?
- And which of those points are the main points?
- How are they connected?
- What points are important to the other party?

9. What concessions can you demand from the other party?
- At what point are you prepared to offer concessions?
- What is non-negotiable for you?
- How will you deal with resistance?
- At which point will you stop the virtual negotiation?

10. How well prepared are you personally?
- How confident do you feel when negotiating?
- What are your triggers, where are you particularly sensitive?
- What will you do if the negotiation breaks down?
- How much time do you want to invest in preparation?

VIRTUAL NEGOTIATION. BEST PRACTICE

Have the checklist for virtual negotiations ready in your meeting; an open window on a second screen works well for this. This way you can always take a look at your basic principles. Write down spontaneous observations, such as questions that arise from the situation or that you would like to ask. The clattering of your keyboard in the background disrupts communication.

Once you have prepared yourself using the checklist for virtual negotiations, you can plan your virtual negotiation approach. In the following recommendations, you will learn about the tactics behind the cooperative and competitive negotiation styles and how to adapt them to remote negotiations. You can find out more in the book *Besser verhandeln. Das Trainingsbuch* by Jutta Portner.

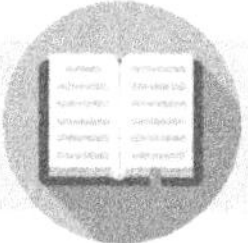

VIRTUAL NEGOTIATION. READING MATERIAL

Jutta Portner
Besser verhandeln
Das Trainingsbuch

GABAL Verlag
392 Seiten
23,0 x 15,5 cm

978-3-86936-054-6
€ 32,90 (D) | € 33,90 (A)

VIRTUAL NEGOTIATION. KNOWLEDGE

The negotiation dilemma

You are now familiar with the competitive and cooperative negotiation styles and the two basic ways of creating value and claiming value. The distribution of resources plays a decisive role here. "I want my piece of the pie and as much of it as possible!" is the basic attitude of competitive negotiators, while the motto of cooperative negotiators is "How can I enlarge the pie, or how can I distribute the pie fairly if I can't enlarge it?"

In which constellation can different negotiation styles come together?
Mathematically, there are three possibilities:

- Competitive meets competitive.
- Competitive meets cooperative.
- Cooperative meets cooperative.

What are the results of such negotiations?
- Competitive versus competitive: The two styles negotiate hard, sometimes with losses for both sides, or fail to reach a result because nobody wants to give in.
- Competitive versus cooperative: Hard beats soft, because soft accepts demands and gives in to achieve an outcome.
- Cooperative and cooperative: Achieve a result that is good for both sides.

What does this mean specifically for an individual negotiator?
1. Best case: I negotiate competitively, the other side negotiates cooperatively – I thereby claim the value that the other side has created.
2. Second-best case: I negotiate cooperatively, and so does the other side – both sides create value and divide it up between themselves.
3. Third-best case: I negotiate competitively, as does the other side – both sides claim value, but create little value.
4. Worst case: The other side negotiates competitively, I negotiate cooperatively – the other side claims the value that I have created.

What is the negotiation dilemma?
The term "negotiation dilemma" is based on the "prisoner's dilemma." The paradox that is a central component of game theory[19] shows that individually self-interested decisions can lead to collectively worse outcomes. One party cannot be put in a better position without simultaneously putting another party in a worse position. For the negotiator, this means that cooperative negotiation is always only the second-best option, as the best option for the individual is to claim the value that the other has created, i.e. to be competitive oneself while the other is yielding. This may work once, but not in longer-term cooperations.

If you want to cooperate and seek a win-win situation

The Harvard Concept has been established as an approach to cooperative negotiation for around 40 years. If your aim is to work with negotiating parties on a long-term basis, it can achieve excellent results. It was developed from Harvard Law School's Program on Negotiation by Roger Fisher and William Ury. In 1981, the book *Getting to Yes* was published, which introduced the method based on five principles to the general public for the first time. The Harvard Concept is the result of years of research, all aimed at determining which principles negotiators apply to achieve mutually satisfactory results in the long term for both sides. What was surprising was that the same recurring principles could always be observed, regardless of whether the negotiations were diplomatic, of a business nature, or with friends and family. This is why "open negotiation based on the Harvard Concept" has become an established practice:

- There is hardly any other concept that is so comprehensive and complete. It incorporates many other well-known and successfully tested approaches and theories.
- The success factors of the Harvard Concept have proven themselves in practice, regardless of the specific circumstances, negotiating parties, and the time.
- Ultimately, it is in the interests of all parties involved to apply the rules of a win-win concept.

Roger Fisher & William Ury
Getting to Yes
Negotiating an Agreement Without Giving In

Penguin
240 Seiten

978-0-14-311875-6

VIRTUAL NEGOTIATION. KNOWLEDGE

The advantages of negotiating based on the Harvard Concept
The consistent application of the principles of the Getting to Yes concept offers a systematic transition …

from:	to:
Haggling over positions	Responding to interests
"Your problem is your problem."	"Your problem concerns me too."
"I'm in control the other party."	"We are in control of the process."
Relationship as leverage	Relationship as a source of cooperation
Concessions lead to compromises	Creativity leads to new possibilities
Good "deal" or good relationship	Good "deal" and good relationship
What one wins, the other loses ("zero-sum game")	Both win ("game with variable quantity")
Strongest person wins	Fair solutions

The Harvard Concept: Principle 1

Differentiate between the topic of the negotiation and the relationship between the negotiating parties. Be gentle with the individual and firm on the issue.

Confusing substantive issues with relationship problems harms the relationship and paralyzes progress in the matter. However, a functioning relationship is a prerequisite for the efficient handling of such issues.

The recommendation is therefore to:

- Recognize relationship problems and treat them separately from substantive issues.
- Review the relationship with negotiating parties for mutual trust, mutual acceptance, and functioning communication. This also means apologizing when mistakes have been made.
- Contact before contract! Work on relationship problems before you start with the substantive issues.
- Build mutual trust by always behaving in a trustworthy manner during the negotiation, regardless of the circumstances or the behavior of the other negotiating party.
- Pursue your objective clearly and consistently. Don't yield just to maintain harmony.

VIRTUAL NEGOTIATION. BEST PRACTICE

The importance of a sound relationship between negotiators is the central message of Principle 1 of the Harvard Concept. In virtual negotiations, negotiators often find it difficult to make contact. Once you have understood the necessity, make sure you invest time in getting to know each other. Remain relaxed and confident.

The Harvard Concept: Principle 2

Focus on interests, not positions.

A negotiating position is understood as a clearly defined demand in a negotiation: "We want ... from you, we need ..., we require ..., we are prepared to pay ... for ..." According to the Harvard Concept, behind every negotiating position lies an interest. Interests are understood as the motives, motivations, as well as the needs and fears of the negotiating parties. These are legitimate concerns of any negotiating party. Interests can often be satisfied by different solutions. In contrast to positional negotiation, interest-based negotiation is therefore open when it comes to a negotiation's outcome and thus creates new and often creative solution possibilities. Taking a position may indicate strength, but it reveals a weakness, as it stems from a fear of leaving the negotiation with a bad result. The longer a position is held, the more difficult it is to move away from it. The road back is then no longer possible in the interests of saving face.

The recommendation is therefore to:

- Be clear about your own interests and ask yourself questions during the preparation phase: What is really important to us?
- State your own interests openly without taking a premature position.
- Question the other party's position with regard to the underlying interests: Why do you need ...? What do you need ... for? Why is ... important to you? Why do you want ...?
- Always focus on common interests first. This establishes common ground. For the time being, put any conflicts of interest to rest and deal with them in a second step.

VIRTUAL NEGOTIATION. KNOWLEDGE

The skill of making proposals

Part of the nature of a virtual negotiation is to resolve a conflict of interest. Otherwise, there would be no need to meet online. One side wants one solution, the other side another. How quickly an agreement is reached depends on the size of the difference between the two proposed solutions, how important it is for both sides to reach an agreement, and how much negotiation power each side holds. According to Huthwaite International, negotiation professionals master the art of skillfully presenting proposals to expedite the agreement. Average negotiators submit a counter-proposal on average 3.1 times per hour, while professional negotiators do so only 1.7 times per hour. What does this mean? Negotiation professionals spend more time exploring the motives and reasons behind the demands of the other party. This knowledge allows them to subsequently make more tailored offers. Remember in your next virtual negotiation to first explore, and then in the second step, propose a solution. This prevents virtual negotiations from going in circles, which can be frustrating for all parties involved.

VIRTUAL NEGOTIATION. BEST PRACTICE

Interests instead of positions! In virtual negotiation, this means working a lot with questions to explore the interests of the other party. Ask plenty of open questions in your virtual negotiation. Explain why you are asking: "Help me to understand why ..." Make frequent short interim summaries to verify your understanding. It is more difficult to endure silence in a virtual space. Nevertheless, pause for a moment if you have asked the other party for further clarification. In larger virtual negotiation groups, agree on a simple gesture, such as raising your hand, if you have additional questions and want to go into more detail. Focus first on the interests of the other party and only communicate your interests in the second step. Don't comment on the interests of others; just let them be. Nobody appreciates having their perspective overanalyzed or dissected.

The Harvard Concept: Principle 3

First devise as many options as possible. Evaluate and make decisions later.

If you want to find a solution in a negotiation that best meets the interests of all parties involved, you need everyone to come up with creative ideas. All too often, negotiators work against one another instead of with one another, and creativity is often hindered by hasty judgments. As a result, there is a risk of taking up positions, irrevocably committing to them, and losing sight of interests. Often, negotiators have only one possible solution in their mind and are satisfied once they have achieved it, so there is not even an attempt to search for a second, third, or fourth possible solution. This approach is based on the assumption that the "pie" is limited and that others should solve their own problems.

The recommendation is therefore to:

- Postpone the negotiation of terms and conditions as far back as possible. Obviously, you want to reach an agreement on the price, but first it's worth exploring other ways to work together.
- Ask questions about possible solutions, ideally stating the interests of the negotiating party first and then your own. "What can we do so that you get ... (interests of the other party) and we get ... (our own interests)?"
- Don't settle for the first best solution; look for additional models or variations. "That sounds interesting. Are there any other options?"

- Focus on possible solutions that take into account the interests of both parties, i.e. that also satisfy the interests of the other party.
- Put off making statements of approval or rejection until the creative potential of everyone involved has been fully tapped.

The Harvard Concept: Principle 4

Resolve conflicts of interest by applying objective criteria and fair procedures.

Conflicts often arise as a result of the conflicting, contradictory interests of the negotiating parties. Ruthlessly asserting one's own interests at the expense of the negotiating party is just as arbitrary as sacrificing one's own interests in favor of the other party. Arbitrariness always leads to bad blood. If you succeed in replacing arbitrariness with transparency, i.e. with comprehensibility, appropriateness, and fairness, then the decisions will be supported by all those involved. Agreements can then be accepted, even if they are not to the absolute satisfaction of one party or the other. Negotiators will only feel that they are on an equal footing with their negotiating parties if they consider the standard applied to be fair.

The recommendation is therefore to: Look for universally applicable norms, values, and legal principles that can be used as objective decision-making criteria because they:

- are independent of all partisan interests of the individual negotiating parties.
- apply to all negotiating parties involved and can therefore be binding.

VIRTUAL NEGOTIATION. BEST PRACTICE

When preparing for your virtual negotiation, consider the facts and standards on which a joint decision can be made. How do you want to evaluate individual options? Would you like a cost breakdown? Do you want to establish a standard with framework agreements? How will you deal with force majeure? Do you require non-competition clauses? How can you find a compromise so that the other party is also satisfied? What compensation options can you offer? It is not easy to come up with all these questions and their answers without thorough preparation. One advantage of virtual negotiations is that you can have quick access to many different variations at any time, especially when it comes to calculations.

The Harvard Concept: Principle 5

Decide for or against a result of a negotiation by comparing it with your best alternative.

A negotiation result is a success if the agreement is better than the best possible alternative. No one will agree to a negotiated solution if there is a better option outside the negotiation table. In this way, the best alternative becomes an independent criterion for or against a negotiation result, irrespective of the other party. The Harvard Concept refers to the best alternative as BATNA, the Best Alternative to Negotiated Agreement. If such an alternative is available, the negotiating parties' sense of dependency is reduced: If you have an attractive plan B, you wield a great deal of negotiating power. In the worst case, if you are negotiating with a monopolist, you wield little or no negotiating power.

The recommendation is therefore to:

- Improve possible alternatives to your current BATNA early on. A company dependent on a monopolist is likely to start recruiting and qualifying other suppliers as soon as possible.
- Only agree to a decision if it is better than your BATNA.
- Check whether the other side has a better alternative to a proposed negotiated solution. This is something you can ask about directly during the negotiation, or you may have already researched it in advance.
- Do not threaten the negotiating party with your own alternative, but rather communicate this as your own decision-making problem.
- Include the second-best alternative of all parties as an option in decision-making processes.

VIRTUAL NEGOTIATION. BEST PRACTICE

Another advantage of virtual negotiation is that you can contact and coordinate with other potential negotiating parties more quickly and easily. The risk of agreeing to a result solely because of the effort already invested is eliminated. Such an approach enhances your understanding of potential alternatives in the market and provides you with a realistic assessment of your situation and the associated negotiating power.

Those who want to cooperate ask.

According to the Huthwaite International study, negotiation professionals spend 41 percent of their time asking questions to understand the thinking behind the perspectives of the other party. In comparison, the group of average negotiators invested only 33 percent of their time in asking questions. Therefore, always be aware of how crucial it is in negotiations to precisely understand what the negotiating partner wants, regardless of whether the other party is trying to pursue their goal with inflexibility or is cooperatively interested in a joint solution. Questioning techniques are the perfect communication tool for this. Many negotiators find it difficult to ask questions, as they spend most of their time talking and trying to make themselves understood. However, negotiation professionals have understood the crucial role that questions play and use skillful questioning techniques frequently. Their average is four questions per 15 minutes of negotiation time. Of course, the type of question matters, as well as whether the responses of the negotiating parties are actively listened to and understood, and then meet with resonance. There are two main types of questions that are generally known: closed and open questions. A negotiator should know the differences and their significance for the negotiation. A closed question can be answered with a simple "yes" or "no." This is why closed questions are also referred to as "decision questions". They do not open a dialogue, but close it by asking for a precise decision. Open questions, on the other hand, invite the negotiating party to reveal their opinions and facts, which is why they are also called "information questions". Negotiators can actively steer the negotiation by consciously using open or closed questions:

- "What is important to you?" – an open question if you want to create clarity
- "What options do we have?" – an open question to come up with solutions
- "Shall we agree on this?" – a closed question, especially when you want to finalize the deal.

And also be aware of one thing: Asking questions also involves listening – like the key to a lock. There are negotiators who become very irritated if they are asked a question but are not listened to when formulating the answer. Such a discrepancy often leads to the repetition of arguments, with the tone frequently changing and the atmosphere becoming heated. This can be the first step towards a dead end, which must be avoided at all costs.

If you want to win and work with tricks

If, as a negotiator, you meet another party that is more dependent on you than the other way around, you will probably have more attractive alternatives available to you in the event of a failure to reach an agreement. You therefore have more negotiating power and can use this imbalance to your advantage. You can engage competitively, while the other party will try to cooperate with you. At first glance, this may seem like a tempting scenario and a comfortable situation for you as the "more powerful" party. You take what the other side gives. In the short term, this competitive approach makes sense because you as the negotiator can focus on maximizing your own gains. In the long term, however, such an imbalance often results in dissatisfaction on the part of the negotiator who emerges from the competition as the loser. It can also happen that negotiating parties learn over time to play the game of competition and set the first offer so high from the outset that there is enough room for a tough back and forth. Last but not least, it doesn't matter how much joy negotiators derive from tough negotiations or how skilled they are in them. Cultural aspects also have an influence on negotiation behavior. People who grow up in bazaar cultures often deal with the competitive style of negotiation much more naturally, as they have been familiar with it since childhood. Virtual negotiators who want to win ask themselves the following questions:

- In which situations is competitive negotiation used?
- How are terms negotiated virtually when the only question is the price?
- How are competitive tricks used in virtual negotiations?

In which situations is competitive negotiation used?

Competitive negotiations usually take place in the case of one-off interactions that will not result in further cooperation. These can include private situations such as real estate purchases, as you are rarely likely to buy a second property from the same agent. The purchase or sale of vehicles would also be such an example. In the business world, the negotiation of terms with suppliers in the project business or company acquisitions or sales are possible situations in which negotiations are exclusively competitive. However, negotiations in which negotiators plan to work together over the longer term can also have a competitive element when it comes to prices and conditions, alongside the cooperative element of joint problem-solving. The company's interest in profit takes precedence at this point, and the nature of the negotiation plays a subordinate role. If the negotiating parties are already familiar with one another, virtual negotiations are often preferred. If larger budgets are being negotiated and the parties do not yet know each other, the decision is usually in favor of face-to-face negotiations.

How are terms negotiated virtually when the only question is the price?

If price is the only argument and you can't enlarge the pie through creativity, then the rules of concession will help you. Here are some recommendations:

- Leave yourself room for concessions.
- Plan the steps in which you will make concessions.
- Make the first offer if the market is non-transparent; this way, you will have dropped the price anchor.
- Let the other party make the first offer if the market is transparent. When in doubt, the rule is that those negotiators who are offering something should name the price first.
- Ask for concessions proactively. If you do not ask, the other party will not voluntarily accommodate you.
- Don't be the first person to make a major concession.
- Object if the other party demands concessions. Verbally express that such a demand is too much for you.
- Set a condition for every concession.
- If you gain a concession, you do not automatically have to offer one.
- Exchange concessions that mean little to you for those that are of high value to you and vice versa.
- If you give, give in small steps.
- Let your concessions get smaller and smaller.
- Take advantage of the power of limited authority: "This is something I can't decide on today" or "Our company philosophy dictates that we need to address this kind of thing internally first."
- Don't feel confident too soon. Nothing is final until the final point has been agreed.

VIRTUAL NEGOTIATION. BEST PRACTICE

One advantage of negotiating terms and conditions in a virtual space is that you can access any notes you have prepared much more easily than in face-to-face negotiations. At any time, you can have a look at your various calculations and exchange information with your team using your secondary communication channel. A potential disadvantage could be that negotiators who are not fond of tough negotiations, even in face-to-face negotiations, may be even less inclined to do so in the virtual space. Here, too, the trap of avoidance is lurking: What is uncomfortable tends to be avoided. A general rule could be to go at least three rounds, i.e. to renegotiate the price three times before you finally agree.

VIRTUAL NEGOTIATION. INTERVIEW

DR. JÖRG ROTTENBURGER

Dr. Jörg Rottenburger completed his doctorate at WHU (Otto Beisheim School of Management) International Business and Supply Management on the topic of "Differentiating Deception: New Insights into Bluffing, Lying and Paltering in Business Negotiations." In 2019, Dr. Jörg Rottenburger was awarded the Science Prize of the German Association of Materials Management, Purchasing, and Logistics (BME) for his dissertation. In his work, he examines the significance of deception in purchasing negotiations. His thesis: In many industries, procurement has become the cornerstone for achieving competitive advantages. This means that purchasing negotiations are becoming increasingly important. His dissertation examines deceptions in such negotiations on the basis of eight negotiation studies involving more than 700 buyers and sellers from Europe and North America. Today, Dr. Jörg Rottenburger works as a Business Process Owner at PERI SE.

J.P. It's alright, it's just a bluff. Is deception in negotiations morally acceptable?

J.R. Yes and no. Generally speaking, different rules apply when it comes to negotiations. However, a distinction must be made here between three types of deception: Omissions, bluffs, and lies.

- An omission is a statement that is true but leaves out essential aspects in order to deliberately mislead the other person into drawing false conclusions.
- Bluffing is defined as making false threats that cannot be carried out and making false statements about one's own negotiating position.
- Lying, on the other hand, includes making false promises, i.e. promises that cannot be kept, and making false statements regarding the topic of the negotiation.

Overall, we can say that bluffs are considered legitimate, omissions fall into a gray area, while lying is considered immoral. The fact that the different types of deception are judged differently is not only due to their differences in substance, but also to how we are able to justify them to ourselves: Bluffs concern things that, according to the prevailing opinion, are none of my counterpart's business anyway – for example, how much profit I will make on a transaction and whether there are any other potential buyers. If, on the other hand, it is a matter of deception about the matter being negotiated – for example, with regard to the functionality of the product to be purchased – internal justification is much more difficult.

J.P. Is it easier to deceive in virtual negotiations?

J.R. Virtual negotiations provide us with more justifications to rationalize deceptive maneuvers to ourselves, as everything feels more distant and impersonal. However, there is a particular risk of creating a self-fulfilling prophecy: If I assume that there will be more deception in virtual contexts, my own threshold of restraint will also be lowered.

J.P. What recommendations can you give to online negotiators?

J.R. Our research shows that the incidence of lies can be reduced, for example, by referring to ethical principles. That's why during the introductions at the beginning of a negotiation, I sometimes casually mention that my employer is a family business with a strong value system.

You can also attempt to make virtual negotiations more personal; for example, I consider turning on the camera and having a round of introductions at the beginning of a new negotiation constellation a must.

In general, however, we should not delude ourselves: Whenever there is a negotiation, sooner or later there will be deception. The important thing is that we can deal with it appropriately. Both offline and online, it is therefore essential to be well prepared and vigilant in order to be able to verify the plausibility of your counterpart's statements during the negotiation. Listen attentively and, in the event of evasive or vague statements, follow up with specific questions until you obtain a clear answer.

———

How are competitive tricks used in virtual negotiations?

The use of virtual negotiation tricks is truly wizardry. Whether Merlin, Gandalf, Miraculix, or Dumbledore – we are all familiar with the famous wizards. As different as they are, they all have one thing in common: they have mastered magical techniques and the art of deception. As negotiators (or spectators at magic shows), we marvel, doubt, and laugh – and sometimes we also fear what may happen. During negotiations, negotiators often reach for their bag of tricks. The most common tricks are used during the negotiation process. Knowing and using negotiating tricks can be helpful, but that doesn't make you a good negotiator. Without a greater goal, a good strategy, and perfect teamwork within the negotiating team, you won't get far with tricks alone. To understand the effect of tricks, you can use the negotiation process as a guide. Throughout the various phases of negotiations, different tricks have proven effective for practitioners.

Gavin Kennedy, author of the bestseller *Everything is Negotiable. How to get the Best Deal Every Time*[20] presents a collection of tricks in this book and in supplementary training materials for students[21]. The tricks can be divided into three areas:

- **Pre-tricks** at the beginning of the virtual negotiation: the opening and the game for power

- **Mid-tricks** during the virtual negotiation: right in the middle of it all, sometimes evident, sometimes not
- **Late tricks** shortly before the conclusion of the virtual negotiation: almost finished, but here's one last surprise

At the beginning of the negotiation, the overture sets the tone. When negotiating competitively many negotiators expect to gain an advantage through dominance. In this case, they are relying on created negotiation power as opposed to inherent negotiation power. As the parties are seen as opponents to be defeated in competitive negotiations, any means that weaken the other party are also permitted. Dominant behaviors manifest in various ways, even early in negotiations, in the form of pre-tricks.

In the middle of a negotiation, people argue and haggle. The pie is divided up. This is where negotiating tricks can help to influence the acceptance of what each negotiator is entitled to. The underlying attitude is "I can make you believe that you are entitled to nothing, or at least less." There is a broad range of mid-tricks that can be used to deceive. From small, subtle, barely noticeable tricks to heavy artillery on the edge of legality, the "dirty tricks."

At the end of the negotiation, in the closing phase, the goal is to reach a final decision. This is where we encounter late tricks that negotiators use to push the other party to conclude a deal in order to gain a final advantage for their own side. Some of the tricks are well known and always work brilliantly. Others are less known.

Everything you need to know about pre-tricks

VIRTUAL NEGOTIATION. BEST PRACTICE

Pre-tricks are used at the beginning of a virtual negotiation. The battle for power already commences in the opening, and this often goes hand in hand with control: control of information, of relationships, of negotiations. Exercising control requires dominance and a strategy of intimidation aimed at making the other party feel smaller than they actually are. This sense of powerlessness results in negotiators not meeting on an equal footing. The strong, powerful side leads, while the weak, powerless side follows. Since the format in virtual negotiations is fixed by equally sized thumbnails, it is difficult to reinforce dominance using body language. The following pre-tricks 1 to 3 can be used to exert influence through the establishment of preconditions, the manipulation of the agenda, and the assertion that certain issues are fundamentally non-negotiable.

VIRTUAL NEGOTIATION. READING MATERIAL

Jutta Portner
Flexibel verhandeln
Die vier Fälle der NEGO-Strategie

GABAL Verlag
360 Seiten
23,0 x 15,6 cm

978-3-86936-755-2
€ 34,90 (D) | € 35,90 (A)

Pre-trick 1: Establishing preconditions

The negotiator can set preconditions even before the actual negotiation and thereby establish conditions that are regarded as set. These could be, for example, exclusivity agreements, demands to transfer IP rights (patent rights), restrictions against working with competitors, letters of intent, and the like. Preconditions are often communicated by email in virtual negotiations.

How can pre-trick 1 be countered? Be wary if such conditions are the prerequisites for sitting down at the negotiating table with you in the first place. However, there are also situations in which preconditions are not tricks, but help the negotiator to avoid bad experiences made in the past from the outset. It is important to pay close attention here. Address the preconditions in the first virtual meeting and question their permanence.

Pre-trick 2: Manipulation of the agenda

An agenda is sent out in advance. The negotiators then start to prepare themselves for the specified topics and framework conditions. Once the virtual negotiation is opened, the other party realizes that the agenda has been changed. As a result, they are either unprepared or poorly prepared, which can benefit those who manipulated the agenda. Sometimes a seemingly friendly yet sham explanation is given and apologies are made for the lack of prior notification of the change of agenda. The other party has no desire to see the tone of the negotiation deteriorate and grudgingly accepts the change. The manipulation of the agenda can also affect the number of negotiators taking part. For example, additional people could be brought in on short notice or – this is where the magic happens – higher-ranking decision-makers could join the team spontaneously or not show up at all.

How can pre-trick 2 be countered? If the agenda has been changed, intervene, as there is a high risk that the other party will attempt to influence the order and prioritization of the points to be negotiated before the opening. Both sides always have the right to a veto when it comes to changing the agenda of the topics to be negotiated. One advantage of virtual negotiations is that new appointments can usually be arranged quickly.

Pre-trick 3: That is a "non-negotiable"

Similar to preconditions, there are also competitive negotiators who declare some negotiation items "non-negotiable" from the outset. They speculate that the other party will simply swallow this bitter pill, not even questioning such a vehemently asserted claim.

How can pre-trick 3 be countered? Whether you accept such conditions without protest or make them an issue depends on your perception of your own negotiating power. How important is this collaboration to you? If you have alternatives, then it is certainly worth making this an issue and including it as a point of negotiation. It also matters how crucial the "non-negotiable point" is to the overall outcome. Depending on their importance, non-negotiables can also become deal breakers. If you are aware of this and see no way to overcome the obstacle, it may make sense to terminate the negotiation early. If the non-negotiable point concerns aspects of lesser value, you, as the negotiator may consider accepting the point or setting it aside temporarily. You can mention that you'll revisit the overall package at a later stage when the negotiation has progressed. Agree with the negotiating parties in virtual negotiations on where you want to set aside open points, determine who will be responsible for them, and specify when you will revisit them. This is one of the tasks of the person facilitating the virtual negotiation.

Everything you need to know about mid-tricks

VIRTUAL NEGOTIATION. BEST PRACTICE

Mid-tricks are used by virtual negotiators during negotiations when it comes to offers, demands, and conditions. It is the dose of tricks that determines their effectiveness. Nowadays, many of the tricks used in face-to-face negotiations are well known. If overplayed, they can have the opposite effect. Negotiators feel tricked, the tone of the negotiation can deteriorate rapidly, and the other party suddenly finds itself constantly on guard. If your mid-tricks are used too early, the other party will know what your intentions are, making you easy to predict. Most of the mid-tricks can be used in both face-to-face and virtual negotiations. One of the main differences is that negotiators in online negotiations need to be more attentive to recognize the tricks and be able to ward them off in the next step. Here, technology clearly favors those negotiating competitively, as a portion of the other party's attention will be tied up in managing the technological aspects of such a negotiation.

VIRTUAL NEGOTIATION. KNOWLEDGE

10 mid-tricks from the professional negotiator's toolbox
Seasoned negotiators often have a big box of tricks and like to pop open the lid several times during virtual negotiations in order to secure concessions for their own benefit without giving much themselves. The ten most common tricks[22] are:

1. The bluff: the oldest trick in the book
2. The flash in the pan: a lot of fuss about nothing
3. Take it or leave it: eat or die
4. The salami tactic: slice by slice
5. Stroking the ego: compliments and more
6. Good guy – bad guy: the carrot and the stick
7. The compassion card: skillfully tugging at the heartstrings
8. The call for a higher authority: negotiations only take place with the boss
9. Split the difference: meeting in the middle
10. The nibble: every little bit counts

Mid-trick 1: The bluff: the oldest trick in the book
Bluffing is the deliberate deception and misleading of negotiating parties and is one of the most common negotiating tricks. You are

probably familiar with the concept from playing cards: You have a lousy hand but let the other party believe the opposite. The aim of a bluff is to force the other party to make concessions on the assumption that a better alternative is available. This often works, but the "bluffer" must be prepared to bear the consequences if the other player doesn't take the bait. The more transparent the market is and the more knowledge a negotiator has about conditions and products, the harder it becomes to bluff. Negotiators often find it easier to bluff in remote negotiations because lying is easier. There is a much greater risk of being exposed by body language signals or a deep look in the eye in face-to-face negotiations.

How can mid-trick 1 be countered? Prepare yourself well and take your chances. The willingness to lose can also make you strong. Sometimes you make a gamble and lose. Every now and then you will fall if you want to get the most out of the negotiation. Generally, it will not be a problem. Different rules apply in negotiations than in real life. Don't expect absolute honesty from your counterpart, but definitely fairness.

Mid-trick 2: The flash in the pan: a lot of fuss about nothing
Unions that call for collective bargaining are masters at making flash-in-the-pan demands. Even in difficult times, unions demand concessions of a high magnitude, knowing very well from the outset that they will never receive them in full: improved retirement benefits, safety bonuses, night shift bonuses, weekend and holiday bonuses, shorter weekly working hours, additional vacation days, and improved working conditions. History shows that some of the demands fade over time and the core demands remain on the table as soon as the flash in the pan dies down. Generally, these are demands that concern job security and salaries. Flash-in-the-pan demands are used to be "sacrificed" to the other party with the knowledge that you will later receive something of greater importance for your own side. In most cases, the other party does not know what is important to the negotiator. Cashing in on flash-in-the-pan demands gives the other party a high level of satisfaction. You can take home an initial victory and sell it as such within your own organization. "Look what we

managed to get out of them, and it really did them in!" In addition, as the flash in the pan goes out, the complexity of the issues is also resolved. This results in the feeling of getting closer to a final agreement.

How can mid-trick 2 be countered? Play the game too. Negotiators can respond in kind and also begin with exaggerated demands. The "flash-in-the-pan" trick is easier to endure virtually; distance can be better maintained in this way. The feeling of being part of a game that is predictable can turn negotiators in the corporate world into industry actors.

Mid-trick 3: Take it or leave it: eat or die

If a negotiator suddenly confronts the other party with the "eat or die" trick in the course of a seemingly well-developing negotiation, this can be tough for the cooperative negotiator. It is important that the demand is credible. If the other party has reasonable doubts about its credibility, this trick will not work.

How can mid-trick 3 be countered? Always stay calm. This is the first immediate measure. The other party wants to put you under pressure and make you fear that you will end up empty-handed. Don't be intimidated; see this trick as the start of a tough battle over the terms and conditions, provided of course that you have an alternative. Under no circumstances should you issue a counter-threat. Even in the face of "take it or leave it," it is easier for virtual negotiators to maintain an emotional distance. In contrast to a face-to-face negotiation, the emotional entanglement triggered by the element of surprise can be kept under control more easily.

Mid-trick 4: The salami tactic: slice by slice

The former President of the European Commission, Jean-Claude Junker, describes the salami tactic as follows: "We decide on something, put it out there, and wait for some time to see if anything happens. If there is no big outcry and no riots, because most people don't even understand what has been decided on, then we carry on. Step by step, until there is no turning back."[23] The salami tactic is metaphorically derived from cutting a salami into individual slices. If a single slice is missing, it is hardly noticeable. But if you cut further and further, the salami will become shorter after a while. Soon afterwards, it has disappeared completely, and in the end, you are full. In virtual negotiations, you can gradually demand small concessions that don't hurt the negotiating party and therefore go almost unnoticed. Then you make the next small demand at the next meeting and again at the next ... In this way, the concessions add up over time.

How can mid-trick 4 be countered? A basic rule of negotiation tactics is that concessions are not given away, but exchanged. Stay focused, especially in virtual negotiations, when you are asked for a small concession. Phrases such as "If we meet you with X, then we want Y in return" ensure that you also get slices of salami and that both sides are satisfied in the end. Alternatively, you can also include small demands for concessions with the note that the procedure should first be clarified internally in order to then evaluate the overall package.

Mid-trick 5: Stroking the ego: compliments and more

Everyone wants to be satisfied. Everyone likes to negotiate when they feel they have won in the end. And sometimes we even wind up getting things that we don't even need. We strive to satisfy our needs, because we want to feel good. Experienced negotiators know that. A very experienced negotiation professional, who conducted important negotiations for a large automotive group for many years, described it like this: "Sell a small concession as the greatest possible pain."

How can mid-trick 5 be countered? Take time to prepare and know your triggers. What buttons does the other party have to press to trigger the desire to want something? Get to know yourself. Is it important to you to bask in the glow of success or to be envied by others? If so, then here, too, you should arrange a follow-up appointment for the next step of the virtual negotiation. Think about the situation calmly before you make decisions that you will regret afterwards.

"Make them happy!": Why it's tactically smart to help the other party get their needs met

Negotiators feel satisfied when …
… they get something that someone else wanted.
… they get a better price than they imagined.
… they get more than they expected.
… they had to fight hard for something or they unexpectedly get something extra.
… others praise them for the deal or envy them for the deal.
… they realize that the other party has made a mistake in their favor.

Mid-trick 6: Good guy – bad guy: the carrot and the stick

Good guy – bad guy is a negotiating trick that many people know from movies. The suspect is questioned and refuses to cooperate. Why should they confess anything to the police? To break the silence, two police officers engage as a team. The bad cop insults the accused, backs them into a corner, confronts them with accusations, perhaps even blinds them with the glare of a lamp, or deprives them of meals, sleep, and rest. After a while, the bad cop leaves the room and the good cop comes in. The good cop treats the suspect with respect. They are courteous and understanding and offer the suspect something to drink. In return, the suspect opens up and tells the police what they want to know. This negotiating trick is also known as "sugar – vinegar" or "white hat – black hat." In negotiations, the good guy – bad guy method even works when the bad guy is not present. It is enough to point out in a friendly manner that the managing director will never sign such a contract – that it still needs to be reworked. Other possible bad guys who don't have to appear at all could be your bank, your accounting department, your lawyer, your customer, the works council, or your partner. You yourself play the role of the one who would want to move forward, but unfortunately … there is a second, decisive, usually higher authority. Sometimes the bad guy isn't even a person at all. Bad guys can be laws, regulations, committees, computer programs, or procedures. Don't forget that these "higher" authorities have always been made by people. The good guy – bad guy trick may sound corny, but in practice it usually works extremely well and leads to really good results.

How can mid-trick 6 be countered? Don't let yourself get rattled and be tempted to make concessions. Good preparation and clarity with regard to the alternatives will help you to avoid making any rash decisions. In virtual negotiations, address the good guy more often and interrupt the bad guy in their flow of speech by raising your hand. Look at the good guy's thumbnail and answer the good guy's questions. You can also ignore the bad guy's comments. If you are already expecting a tough bad guy before the start of the negotiation and want to slow them down or partially immobilize them, then you should also get support and not negotiate alone against a virtual duo.

VIRTUAL NEGOTIATION. KNOWLEDGE

The choreography of the good guy – bad guy trick

1. In preparation for the virtual negotiation, roles are clarified and an alternative communication channel is defined.
2. The good guy opens the virtual negotiation and conducts the small talk, while the bad guy is present but remains silent.
3. The position and demand of the other party are requested by the good guy.
4. The demand is strictly rejected by the bad guy.
5. The bad guy continues to use counter-arguments, while the good guy remains silent.
6. The bad guy continues to apply pressure in their tone and words.
7. The bad guy's behavior deliberately creates a clear antipathy towards the person.

8. Then the good guy cleverly comes into play again at the highest stage of escalation. Indication of the correct point in time is made via the alternative communication channel.
9. The bad guy says goodbye, annoyed, and leaves the virtual meeting.
10. The good guy apologizes for the bad guy's behavior.
11. The bad guy's position is confirmed by the good guy in a friendly tone.
12. The good guy produces the desired result.

Mid-trick 7: The compassion card: skillfully tugging at the heartstrings

There is a lot to moan and complain about: First came the pandemic, then the war in Ukraine, delivery delays, and inflation. The current business situation is difficult, jobs are at risk, the economy is in the dumps, and the industry is in crisis. As a negotiator, you are to be pitied and therefore expect concessions. The compassion card works well when the other party is empathetic and receptive to human need. The "compassion card" trick is less common in virtual negotiations, as online negotiations have a much stronger focus on efficiency than face-to-face meetings.

How can mid-trick 7 be countered? Express your understanding for the difficult situation in which your negotiating party finds itself. Remain in the role of the active listener and do not slip into the role of the empathic listener; this will make it easier for you to return to the matter at hand. Apply the 1st principle of the Harvard Concept and make a distinction between the relationship with the negotiating party and the topic of negotiation. Be sure to remain gentle with the individual and firm on the issue. Pursue your own goals consistently without giving in. Always be aware of your BATNA. Of course, you can always make exceptions to the rule if there is a real need and you want to help.

Mid-trick 8: The call for a higher authority: negotiations only take place with the boss

"If we don't get anywhere here, then I'll contact your managing director/board/supervisory board directly – or perhaps the best lawyer in town or the press?" The intention behind the "call for a higher authority" trick is to gain an advantage by referencing good connections. It's along the same lines as saying: "You'd better meet me halfway before I pull my strings and you get a slap on the wrist." This trick works with negotiating parties who work in hierarchical structures and prefer harmony. Concessions are made in order to avoid conflicts.

How can mid-trick 8 be countered? Go for it! Let the other negotiator contact your managing director/board/.... It is important that you have internal backing and are all pulling in the same direction. Ideally, the higher-ranking person will delegate the request back to you. Then this trick will no longer be tried in future because its effect will have fizzled out. Always conduct negotiations on an equal footing, and if there is an upward escalation, then do so on both sides. One advantage of digital negotiation is that the "higher authority" can be called in more quickly and, if necessary, right at the moment the threat is made, either to calm things down or to back up the negotiator. Sometimes it is enough if the higher authority only joins in for a short period of time.

Mid-trick 9: Split the difference: let's meet in the middle

This is an ingenious trick. A typical process for negotiating conditions looks like this: One side communicates its demand, whereupon the counterbid is made. Usually, negotiators now start negotiating back and forth until they meet in the middle. Both sides accommodate each other to roughly the same extent. The "let's meet in the middle" trick, which is suggested by one party after the other party has already made an initial major concession, is different. It seems fair – we'll meet in the middle – and it would have been, if a substantial concession had not already been made on the one side.

How can mid-trick 9 be countered? When it comes to dividing up the pie, you have to be careful: Fair means that both sides are approaching each other on an equal footing. Chris Voss has a more nuanced view of the "meeting in the middle" approach. In his bestselling book *Never Split the Difference*[24], the former FBI consultant on hostage negotiations writes that this strategy leads to a good working atmosphere and makes negotiators feel comfortable. In reality, however, it shows that negotiators were too comfortable to engage with what the other party really wanted. According to Voss, this requires listening to one another, treating the opinions presented with respect, and analyzing what the other party really wants, which means more work than a quick run of haggling. When it comes to virtual negotiations, it's all about getting out of the efficiency trap and communicating the added value of taking your time.

Mid-trick 10: The nibble: every little bit counts

A "nibble" is a small morsel that the negotiator gives to the other party during, at the end, or even after the negotiation when agreements are implemented. The advantage of this is that the negotiating parties experience a slightly good feeling. Nibbling also works in the opposite direction. Negotiators get themselves a nibble so that they can gain a small advantage that is not really worth mentioning. Car dealers, for example, have a large stock of nibble items that they can include. But they only do so if customers ask. If you don't ask, you don't win. There are car buyers who, as soon as their dealer prepares the contract, ask for winter floor mats, summer tires, the next higher rim model, lower interest rates, additional service, a full tank of gas when they take delivery of the vehicle, or free delivery of the vehicle to their home. They never get everything for free, but they always get one or two things. Shoppers get nibbles from sellers, and sellers get nibbles from shoppers. People are nibbling everywhere you go. It is a common practice and the nibble is a well-known negotiating tactic. Many negotiators therefore plan from the outset what the nibble will be, the morsel that satisfies the appetite. And then they offer it to the other side as a bonus in the negotiation. Nibbling is more difficult in a virtual environment, especially when such small favors are tangibles. In contrast, there are the non-tangibles such as payment terms, contract durations, and discounts that are easier to nibble on in virtual negotiations.

How can mid-trick 10 be countered? There are two ways to handle nibbling. The first way is to be prepared and include the nibbling in the calculation from the outset; this way, an additional small offer will not be defined as a "loss," but will be part of the negotiation package. The second approach is to pause for a moment and pretend to think: "Oh, I thought we had already closed the deal?" If the nibbler continues to inquire, communicate that you will officially incorporate requests from your side as well, because there's no concession without a counter-concession.

Everything you need to know about late tricks

VIRTUAL NEGOTIATION. BEST PRACTICE

Late tricks are pulled out of your hat shortly before the deal is concluded. This is where negotiators think they have already reached their goal but are then confronted with unexpected surprises in the final stretch. Once again, pressure is exerted to gain a one-sided advantage. The negotiator's expectations are high: to close the deal and go home with an acceptable result. From this perspective, the final phase of the negotiation is a critical moment. Negotiators tend to give away final concessions so as not to risk the overall success of the negotiation in the home stretch. Competitive negotiators are aware of this and will take advantage of it.

Late trick 1: The "quivering quill"

Gavin Kennedy calls the following trick the "quivering quill": You have been negotiating for hours, and it was a give and take. You have come to a result that both sides can live with. Now you meet to sign the contract, but at the last moment there is an additional demand.

How can late trick 1 be countered? In a virtual environment, our "quills" have long since stopped shaking. Instead, one last surprising email flutters into your inbox, or you find a late, unexpected call on your phone. Here, too, you have two alternatives: Either you bite the bullet because you don't want to reopen the can of worms, and you value the conclusion itself more than the gains you could obtain through renegotiation. Or, alternatively, you make it unmistakably clear that the belated demand is a no-go for you. Then it's back to square one for both parties, and you go for another round.

Late trick 2: "Now or never"

Ending a negotiation with the "now or never" trick exerts massive pressure on the other party, which is why it is often referred to as the "walk out" trick. If the other party says "Everything has to be finalized by tomorrow evening at 6 p.m., otherwise I'm out," then the announcement of the deadline is used as a means of exerting pressure. The difficult thing is to assess whether the deadline corresponds to the facts or whether it is being used to create an artificial form of pressure. If you show that you are prepared to break off a negotiation if your counterpart does not accept a deadline, you increase your negotiating power. If your counterpart is trying by all means to override the deadline, you know that you still have a lot to gain. If you use the now or never trick, you must also be prepared to accept the consequences if the other person does not agree to your demand. There is rarely a way back. It would involve a considerable loss of face. Use the now or never trick very rarely, as it is basically a sign of weakness and has an air of immaturity about it. The more often you use the now or never trick, the less seriously you will be taken.

How can late trick 2 be countered? The most skillful way is to ignore it. Often there is an emotional overreaction behind it, and the aggressor is sorry shortly afterwards. Not engaging prevents the issue from escalating further. Instead, ask how this deadline came about and what options are available if the deadline is missed. In virtual negotiations, there is a risk of ending the negotiation quickly, simply by clicking. The now or never trick is about enduring the conflict-laden situation and redirecting it into a constructive negotiation dialogue.

Late trick 3: Time pressure and delay, or: who determines the time, dominates

By building up time pressure, a negotiator can cause the other party to make hasty decisions and not take enough time for research and internal agreements. Delaying decisions, on the other hand, is used as a tactic when you know that the other party needs certain products or services in a time-critical manner and that the delay will put them at a significant disadvantage. This means that negotiating parties are forced to agree to conditions that they would not have agreed to without the added time pressure.

How can late trick 3 be countered? Stay calm and make it clear that although you are currently dependent and realize this, in the long term you will turn to alternatives if the negotiating party is not reliable. If the other party is using the delay trick, it's easier to keep at it in a virtual environment and follow up and knock with friendly audacity until you are heard.

VIRTUAL NEGOTIATION. BEST PRACTICE

Get used to seeing virtual negotiation tricks used by the other party not as a threat, but as a warning to you. This keeps you informed about the other party's true intentions and helps you learn about their attitude and motivation with regard to future cooperation.

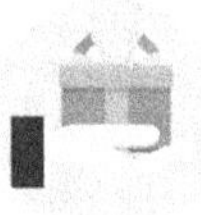

VIRTUAL NEGOTIATION. TIP #21

When difficulties arise online

If difficulties arise in face-to-face negotiations, this can pose a major challenge for negotiators. If a negotiation takes place in a virtual space, a problematic situation is all the more serious. It almost seems as if the virtual environment acts like a burning glass, igniting difficulties more quickly and accelerating the blaze. In addition to the Harvard Concept, there is a second concept that builds on the success of *Getting to Yes* and refers to its principles. In *Getting Past No*[25] the American negotiation expert William Ury uses a five-stage model as a framework, similar to the standard work. It identifies barriers to cooperation and presents principles for overcoming these barriers. The five barriers are:

1. Our emotions get the better of us
2. The other party's emotions are running high
3. The stubbornness of the other party leads to stagnation
4. The other party's dissatisfaction with possible solutions
5. The power of the other party to block the deal

Imagine the following day of negotiations:

07:30 a.m.: During the weekly virtual team meeting, you get into an argument with your assistant about whether to introduce one or two days of remote work for the team. Your assistant pesters you: "Are you crazy, two days working from home? They'll just walk all over us!"

09:00 a.m.: You dial in on time for your next meeting. Your supervisor arrives ten minutes late. You want to make a suggestion on how you can document the results of your research department more easily. Over the weekend, you prepared a presentation and will share it. Your boss looks at it briefly and just waves it off: "It looks like there is still work to be done with that. Next item on the agenda."

2:30 p.m.: In the afternoon, you have an online meeting with a new customer to finalize a contract for the construction of a new plant that has been in preparation for six months. She then says: "Oh, I'm really very sorry, but our CFO has vetoed it. He won't give the okay until you reduce your price by another ten percent."

5:30 p.m.: On the train ride home, you receive an email from management that the ten percent discount for the new customer will not be approved, but "you'll figure it out. We're quite sure of that."

8:00 p.m.: You have decided to watch the current Champions League football game after a day like today when your assistant calls to discuss the topic from earlier, as there seems to be more to it.

You have probably experienced similar days and know the emotional state you finds yourself in after such a marathon of unsatisfactory results. Anger, annoyance, frustration, and rage dominate our feelings. Everyone has to deal with petulant colleagues, rebellious assistants, unruly, inattentive superiors, or unyielding business partners. When we're stuck, when nothing is progressing, and the result is heading towards zero, it's often a clear declaration of war. What can you do? Love it, change it, leave it, or stay unhappy? No one loves difficult situations, and solving problems on your own is usually not very promising. Running away is also not an option. The only choice you have left is collaborative problem-solving. This is exactly where the principle from *Getting Past No* comes in.

VIRTUAL NEGOTIATION. READING MATERIAL

William Ury
Getting Past No
Negotiating In Difficult Situations

Random House
208 Seiten

978-0-553-37131-4

Why negotiators don't cooperate

According to William Ury, there are four reasons why negotiators are not willing to cooperate and why they see negotiating parties as opponents:

1. Negotiators are afraid of cooperation.
2. Negotiators do not know how cooperative negotiation works.
3. Negotiators see no advantage for themselves in cooperative behavior.
4. Negotiators know that they are the more powerful ones.

Negotiators are afraid of cooperation

Negotiators in particular who believe that negotiating successfully means winning think they have to be tough and outsmart the other person. They fear that if they cooperate, they might fail in front of themselves or others. They are afraid of not living up to the expectations placed on them as the "tough guy." The fear of perceived failure then makes them stick to their unwavering, tough negotiating style.

Negotiators do not know how cooperative negotiation works

How can you negotiate cooperatively if no one has ever shown you how? How do you know that individual interests are the driving force behind every position if you have never been told? How do you expect to find solutions together if you have been taught that the "more powerful person dictates the result"? How do you want to negotiate cooperatively if your belief is "Negotiating means defeating your opponent"?

Negotiators see no advantage for themselves in cooperative behavior

From a very early age, we are conditioned in our individualistic society to believe that the strong receive more recognition than the weak. At sports events, those with the highest points receive a trophy, while the others receive a certificate of participation. The person who answers the most questions right wins the quiz. The most popular student is elected class representative, and the best piano player is allowed to perform on the grand piano. We are taught to assert ourselves, to compete, to be better than others, without any ifs or buts. So, it's no wonder that it seems strange at first when the interests of both sides have to be satisfied in business life.

Negotiators know that they are the more powerful ones

Why should you cooperate with someone if you are in a more power-ful position? In many negotiation situations, negotiators do not think about cooperation because they know from the outset that they have more power and can ultimately get what they want or dictate the terms. The negotiating party is dependent and has no alternatives.

In the previous considerations on why negotiators avoid cooper-ation, you learned why negotiations can escalate. What tools do you have at your disposal for de-escalation and a return to constructive communication? The *Getting Past No* concept recommends the follow-ing five principles for turning opponents back into partners:

1. Instead of reacting, reflect.
2. Instead of arguing, change your perspective.
3. Instead of rejecting positions, reformulate them.
4. Instead of exerting pressure, build the Golden Bridge.
5. Instead of bringing opponents to their knees, it is better to bring them to their senses.

Problem 1: Our emotions overwhelm us

One word leads to another, one party starts to become unobjective, and then the others jump on the bandwagon, allow themselves to get provoked, and shoot back. They no longer listen to the arguments of the others. They become loud, impertinent, and hurtful. It no longer has anything to do with the matter at hand. You try everything to de-fend your own point of view loudly, or you react with irony or even sarcasm. What happens in such situations? Your emotions take over. You react without thinking and try to get back at the other party, the whole time trying to one-up them. The spiral of rage winds higher and higher. The situation escalates, and the parties either retaliate or give in with frustration. This is where principle 1 of *Getting Past No* comes in: The natural reaction to an attack, whether it is a personal one or one that has to do with the matter at hand, is either to fight back in the same way or to give in and respond to the demands. Both are unattractive options that lead to dissatisfaction and frustration. Here, William Ury proposes a third option: to calmly suspend or postpone negotiations or discussions in order to regain a cool head.

Here are some typical tactics according to William Ury, to which negotiators react emotionally:

1. The other party's tactic of stonewalling
2. Intimidating the other parties through offensive attacks
3. Trying to outsmart the other parties with negotiating tricks

Getting Past No concept. Principle 1

Don't react. Go to the balcony.

In many cases, the negotiator runs the risk of becoming part of the game of provocation through their reaction. The risk of being drawn into a vicious circle is high. Therefore, the first step is not to react, but to get your own behavior under control. "Go to the balcony," says Ury.

Here are some steps you can take:

- Take a deep breath.
- Take a break.
- Mentally take a step back and review your own areas of weakness (triggers).
- Don't get loud. Don't become unreasonable.
- Reflect on your opponent's tricks (name the game).
- Take time to slow down the discussion to keep your eyes on the prize.

In stressful situations, you can prevent a relapse into old patterns by becoming aware of what have always been innate reactions to emotional pressure from negotiators and then deciding to step out of the game of action and reaction. Emotional reactions to stress are always intuitive and not rational. People react to provocation in three different ways: They fight back, i.e. they fight and defend themselves. In virtual negotiations, they get loud and attack others personally or with regard to the matter at hand. A second innate reaction is to give in so as not to jeopardize peace and harmony. In virtual negotiations, negotiators may retreat into their shell and no longer take part in the negotiation, perhaps even switching off the camera. The third innate reaction is to break off negotiations, i.e. people withdraw from the unpleasant situation by leaving the negotiation with a click of their mouse. All three reactions are destructive. As a result of these immediate reactions, conflicts escalate, virtual negotiators agree even though they don't want to, or inadequate results are achieved. The recommendations of the *Getting Past No* concept can be wonderfully applied to virtual negotiations.

Problem 2: The other party's emotions are running high

But it's not just our *own* emotions that get in the way of negotiating. The emotions of the other party can also be a hindrance. Even if you manage to remain calm, it doesn't mean that your counterpart will be able to remain calm and composed. You may therefore also be shocked to see how the other party becomes increasingly angry, impertinent, and loud or even uses tricks. Principle 2 of *Getting Past No* describes how you can help bring your negotiating party back down to earth in such a situation.

Getting Past No concept. Principle 2

Disarm them. Step to their side.

If you are attacked by negotiating parties, they will intuitively expect you to counterattack or retort. The temptation is great. But instead of getting involved in the argument now, the recommendation is to listen, confirm their arguments, and find as much common ground as possible. This generates a "cognitive dissonance" in the other person, as you are actually perceived as an opponent, but begin to become "likeable" through this behavior. This makes it easier to express your own views clearly without being provocative and creates a favorable climate for discussion.

Here are some steps you can take:

- Listen actively: Paraphrase what you have understood and ask the other party to correct anything you may have forgotten.
- Show that you are following the other party's argument and give them enough time to make their case.
- Agree wherever possible and pile up the "yeses."
- Apologize if necessary.
- Always exude confidence.
- Acknowledge the other side's argumentation.
- Take a stand without provoking, don't say "But ..."; instead, say "Yes, and ..."
- Look at any differences with optimism.

Enemies never establish a rapport

In order to be able to negotiate effectively, you first need to create a pleasant negotiating atmosphere. One common mistake in discussions and negotiations is that both partners only focus on their part and their interests. Active listening makes negotiating easier. This also includes finding as much common ground as possible and being able to appreciate the negotiation or discussion partner as a person. This can dispel the other person's fears, doubts, and anger. Behave exactly opposite to what is expected of you as an opponent.

The ability to deliberately prevent escalations

Negotiation professionals are less likely to find themselves in negotiations that escalate. Huthwaite International investigated the reasons for this and found that negotiation professionals are less likely to do things that make the other party feel provoked. At the same time, behaviors were also observed that were used preventively to avoid escalation. The good news: Nevertheless, 77 percent of all negotiators generally refrain from personal attacks in order to avoid escalation. Many negotiators find it more difficult not to defend themselves immediately when they are attacked by the other party. If there are too many counterattacks, the impression is created that the other party is simply trying to justify themselves or is looking to blame the other party, which in turn can lead to an escalation. Phrases such as "You can't blame us for that," "You cheated, not us," or "You started blaming us first" quickly lead to spiraling escalation. It's not that negotiation professionals don't use these phrases. It's just that they do it about three times less than the average experienced negotiator.

VIRTUAL NEGOTIATION. BEST PRACTICE

Use "I" instead of "you" statements when you want to convey your views in virtual negotiations. The reaction of negotiating parties to "you" statements is that they often feel personally attacked. It is much more difficult to perceive the impact virtually through the thumbnail than in face-to-face negotiations.

Look out for irritating trigger words!

If counterattacks are deliberately suppressed, the number of irritating phrases increases. What does this mean? In contrast to direct attacks, irritating trigger words have a much subtler effect. If negotiators emphasize their honest intentions too often, this makes the other party suspicious. Distrust and skepticism begin to grow. Negotiators wonder why the other party has to emphasize so much how sincere they are. Irritating trigger words are phrases that emphasize your own offering in an exaggeratedly positive way. The following phrases are sure to make negotiators sit up and take notice:

- "What we're offering is really generous"
- "This is a really fair proposal"
- "We just want to take a reasonable approach"
- "To be truly honest, here we'd like to emphasize ..."

Professional negotiators are about four times less likely to use irritating trigger words.

Problem 3: The stubbornness of the other party leads to stagnation

You want to bring the negotiation to a conclusion, but the other party is being stubborn! They're being inflexible, repeating themselves, and not willing to compromise! Does this sound familiar? Principle 3 of *Getting Past No* describes what you can do in these situations: "Behind opposing positions lie common and compatible interests as well as conflicting ones. We tend to assume that just because the other party's position is contradictory, their interests are also contradictory. And if it is in our interest to defend ourselves, then it must be in their interest to attack us. In many negotiations, however, a thorough examination of the underlying interests will reveal the existence of far more shared or compatible interests than those that are in opposition."[26]

Don't reject – change the game.

In order to find a solution in difficult negotiation/discussion situations, the context must be changed. Instead of rejecting your partner's position – which usually only leads to it becoming stronger – joint attention should be focused on the effort to reconcile mutual interests. "Yes, it is difficult to find a solution here. So what can we do? Do you have any ideas?" It is important to focus on the problem by asking about the partner's motivations and their suggestions for advice and solutions. This can also put the partner's position into a new context.

Here are some steps you can take:

- Abandon any stonewalling tactics. Stubbornness can be circumvented by simply ignoring it to see if partners are bluffing with their inflexibility. It can be reinterpreted and the lack of flexibility can be addressed as one behavioral option among many. "You say you won't give us an inch. Let's leave it at that. Where else do you see opportunities for ...?"
- Ignore attack tactics. You can see personal attacks as attacks that address the problem or even define them as opportunities for the future. "What can we do to prevent this from happening to us again?"
- Expose trick attacks. Tricks can be put into a new context by asking clarifying questions, turning the trick against the partners themselves, or by playing along without the other party knowing and thus turning their tricks to your own advantage. "I see that you are working with a time limit here. What happens if we haven't made a decision by the deadline?"
- If these attempts to find a new context are unsuccessful, the problem can be addressed directly and an attempt can be made to steer the negotiation/discussion away from the problem and towards the rules of negotiation/discussion by talking about the method of communication. "We've been going around in circles for 20 minutes. What do you suggest we can do to move forward?"

- Negotiate the ground rules of your negotiation.
- Rephrase a "you" and an "I" into a "we."
- Show that you are happy about the change in atmosphere when it comes to a turning point.

Problem 4: The other party's dissatisfaction with possible solutions

Imagine there are four of you working in a team. When you were hired, you all signed a mobility clause stating that the company can assign you to any location around the world. Now the time has come. One of the four of you has to go to Ulan Bator in Mongolia for two years. Your manager has decided to let the team make the decision themselves. You sit together and your three colleagues quickly agree that you are the right person for the job. They explain to you in detail why you and not the others have to go. Will you go? Probably not! Because you are dissatisfied with the solution. Principle 4 of *Getting Past No* describes what can be done to motivate the other party to come to an agreement. Obstacles to your agreement may be:

- The idea came from the other party.
- The other party does not see its interests satisfied in the solution.
- The other party is afraid of losing face.
- The result came too quickly.

Getting Past No concept. Principle 4

Make it easy to say yes. Build them a golden bridge.

Even if the first three steps have been taken and nothing objectively stands in the way of a solution, the agreement can still fail. The partner may have the feeling of being taken by surprise, as a solution seems to have been found surprisingly quickly, or they may have the impression of losing face to the outside world if they agree to the surprising solution. William Ury proposes the "golden bridge," which should make it as easy as possible for the partner to agree.

Here are some steps you can take:

- Instead of pushing partners to conclude the negotiation/discussion quickly, sit back and let them take the final step across the "golden bridge."
- Building a "golden bridge" involves more than just an attractive offer. It is especially important to involve partners in the decision-making process.
- Even if the agreement was worked out by one side, the end solution should always be a "we" decision.
- Look beyond the other party's obvious interests (such as money) and include other interests such as recognition and autonomy.
- Make sure you find a solution that allows both sides to save face and make the deviation from the initial position plausible to the outside world.
- The "golden bridge" must enable both sides to present the solution as a victory.
- And last but not least, it should be noted that the time factor plays a significant role in negotiations/discussions. It is important both for the partners' own perception and for the outward appearance that a solution is not found too slowly or too quickly.

VIRTUAL NEGOTIATION. BEST PRACTICE

The speed with which a counteroffer is made has an effect on the negotiating climate. If counteroffers come too quickly, they are treated with caution by the other party. Negotiators are perceived as either not receptive or fundamentally opposed. This increases the risk of escalation. The virtual negotiation professional takes their time and holds back from making an immediate counteroffer. They try to understand before they make themselves understood. According to Huthwaite International, average negotiators are twice as likely to make quick counter-proposals.

Problem 5: The power of the other party to block the deal

The last and highest hurdle on the road to cooperation is the problem when the other party knows that they are the more powerful ones and have no interest in negotiating or accommodating you. What can you do to free yourself from the trap of the power game?

Getting Past No concept. Principle 5

Make it hard to say no. Bring them to their senses, not to their knees.
If the "golden bridge" is built and the other party still doesn't want to cross it, it may be because they know that they are more powerful and will get what they want in the end anyway, as the other party is too dependent or has no alternative. The natural reaction of most people will be to intensify the efforts with all their might and to work towards a conclusion at all costs. As the chances of beating the other party at their own game are slim, the weaker party's only option is to bring the stronger party to its senses. According to Ury, the aim of escalated situations is not to defeat partners, but to "win them over."
The recommendation is therefore:

- Reiterate the impact of a "no" by making the consequences crystal clear for the other party.
- Ask questions about "What happens after an agreement is rejected?"
- Warn the other party about the consequences and appeal to the responsibility that will fall on the person accountable for the failure.
- Demonstrate your own BATNA without being provocative to show the other party that you also have alternatives.
- Reconfirm the relationship with the other party and leave the final decision of "no" to them.
- Use the potential of third parties. Form coalitions. Forge alliances. This is often quicker virtually than in person.
- Ask third parties to act as mediators.

- Ask for neutral persons who can facilitate the negotiation.
- Make plans for the long term.
- Always emphasize the value of cooperation. Plan personal visits outside of virtual meetings.

VIRTUAL NEGOTIATION. BEST PRACTICE

Make it difficult for the other party to say no, even in online negotiations. The *Getting Past No* concept is essentially based on taking a step back and keeping your emotions in check. It encourages you to listen instead of talking, to ask questions instead of giving answers, and to bridge differences when the temptation to reinforce your own position is great. The strategy suggests an indirect way to achieve the goal of reaching an agreement not by breaking through the other party's resistance, but by circumventing it and acting contrary to its expectations in order to build cognitive dissonance. Rather than changing the position of the other party, the strategy is aimed at changing the perception of the environment or context. The aim is to turn adversaries into partners. The focus is not on convincing one another, but on finding a joint solution to the problem. Therefore, never ever slam the door in online negotiations, but take advantage of the easy opportunity in the virtual space to meet frequently. This will give you the opportunity to strategically recalibrate in between and start with a new focus on de-escalation.

In Chapter 6, you learned how you can exert influence in virtual negotiations. You now know how to apply the principles of the Harvard Concept and how to use or fend off classic negotiation tactics and tricks, depending on the situation. Write down two things that already work well for you and two things that you can do even better in your online meetings in cooperative and competitive negotiations.

Tip #18: Develop the suitable dramaturgy

....

Tip #19: If you want to cooperate and seek a win-win situation

....

Tip #20: If you want to win and work with tricks

....

Tip #21: When difficulties arise online

....

+ Two things that work well for me:

....
....

- Two things I can do even better next time:

....
....

CHAPTER 7. Never Lose Sight of the Big Picture – The Fundamental Rules of Virtual Negotiation

In Chapter 7, you will learn how to keep the reins in your hand and not lose control at any point during virtual negotiations. The best way is to lead an online negotiation from the very beginning. To do so, you can utilize the first-mover advantage. Being very familiar with the technology will enable you to handle potential pitfalls with ease, allowing you to focus your attention entirely on the topic at hand without stress. You can help both your side and the other party's negotiators if you use collaborative tools to visualize key content. Miro, Mural, and Conceptboard have proven effective. Last but not least, it will help you to delegate some of the tasks involved in facilitating a virtual negotiation to co-facilitators. Tip 25 explains which tasks you can delegate and which should definitely remain under your control so that you can always maintain an overview. And if you don't have a co-facilitator available, all the recommendations also apply to the facilitator themselves.

VIRTUAL NEGOTIATION. TIP #22

Leading right from the start: Utilize the first-mover advantage

Deepak Malhotra is a professor at Harvard Business School who specializes in negotiation strategy and the author of two major works on negotiation, *Negotiation Genius*[27] and *Negotiating the Impossible*[28]. In *Negotiation Genius*, Malhotra deals with how negotiators can identify opportunities when the other party is not interested, how to get to the truth when the other party is trying to cover it up, as well as how to negotiate from a weak position and exert influence without manipulation. His compass, which guides his negotiating behavior, is always ethical and morally upright. In *Negotiating the Impossible*, he sheds light on the dynamics behind difficult negotiations. What lies at the root of negotiations that escalate? Why do negotiators become aggressive? Why are there situations in which no one is prepared to give an inch? His most important recommendation: leading from the very beginning and taking advantage of the first-mover advantage. What does that mean? Malhotra identifies three methods for getting out of deadlocked situations:

1. The power of framing
2. The power of process
3. The power of empathy

The power of framing, or the art of being the first person to set the direction

Understanding the power of framing when conducting negotiations means being aware of the fact that the person who first exerts influence will have a strong impact on the objectives in the minds of the negotiating parties. If the main speaker sends signals from the outset that point in the direction of cooperation, there is a high probability that undecided partners will follow the given direction and also want to cooperate. The reverse is also true. If you send out signals that your negotiation is about winning and losing, others will most likely follow your lead. How do negotiators become first movers?

- The side that presents its proposal first gains influence through the anchor effect.
- Remember what the presentation of the negotiation result will look like to the other party when they present it to their client or superior.

- Consider the optics of the deal and give the other party something they can take as a success to sell internally.
- When explaining your proposals, always provide your negotiating partners with arguments that they can use to understand your point of view during the negotiation and to explain to those responsible later.
- Create a safe space where asking for assistance regarding the optics of the deal is encouraged. "Help us out. How are we supposed to explain this to our superiors?"
- Turn your attention away from hot topics to other issues that also need to be addressed.
- However, be careful not to belittle yourself and apologize for suggestions or demands.
- Also discuss the negotiating style and structure, not just the content.

VIRTUAL NEGOTIATION. BEST PRACTICE

Especially in virtual negotiations, negotiating parties are often grateful when someone takes the initiative. If you recognize the importance of the first-mover advantage, seize the opportunity to make an impact. This is particularly easy if you are the inviting party; then it goes hand in hand with your role as facilitator. However, even if the other party has invited you, you can be the first person to comment on the fundamental question of how you want to negotiate.

The power of process, or why those who control the process hold the reins

Professional negotiators prepare themselves for the negotiation process as well as the topic and have it down to a tee. That means not only following the seven steps from preparation to follow-up, but also negotiating the implementation of a possible result. Who will do what and by when? Consider the following recommendations for managing the process:

- Whoever determines the time dominates: Always pay attention to time management.
- Negotiate the process first, and only then dive into the depths of the intricacies of the matter at hand.
- Propose a course of action with regard to the process and synchronize this as far as possible and repeatedly with the other party.
- Look for consent that is clear and public. Even if you are unable to obtain consent, this is also important information for you.
- "Nothing is agreed until everything is agreed." The maxim that nothing is fixed until the deal is finalized gives your negotiating parties the security to make proposals in the knowledge that they can still be withdrawn.
- Do not force the other party to be absolutely transparent. Allow your negotiating partners to take time to discuss and decide on the approach and implementation in privacy.
- Be careful that negotiations concerning the process do not turn into proxy wars for negotiating power. Insist on principles of fairness that apply to both sides.

VIRTUAL NEGOTIATION. BEST PRACTICE

Get into the habit of talking about the process at the beginning of each virtual negotiation and gradually develop more agreement and ground rules on how to proceed together. The advantage is that the other party will not overreact if there are interruptions or delays. Utilize the first-mover advantage in your virtual negotiation to think one step ahead and create a framework for future deals.

The power of empathy, or why controlling your emotions helps to de-escalate even the ugliest conflicts

Empathy in negotiation makes it possible to put yourself in other people's shoes, understand their needs, and react accordingly. By trying to put themselves in the other person's shoes, negotiators can build trust and understanding, which in turn leads to better cooperation and a successful outcome. Without empathy, negotiators risk upsetting or alienating the other side, which can lead to poor results or even escalation. From this perspective, empathy expands the options that negotiators have for resolving conflicts. Empathy enriches the toolbox of professional negotiators if it is used consciously and purposefully. You should therefore consider the following:

- Empathy is most in demand with negotiating parties who seem to deserve it the least.
- The more seemingly incomprehensible the other party's behavior is, the greater the potential benefit of understanding it.
- Consider what the best compromise is between maintaining your strategic flexibility on the one hand, and preserving your credibility on the other. It requires a certain degree of sensitivity to achieve this balancing act.
- Be careful with unnecessary ultimatums and threats. This will back the other party into a corner. The response to this will be attack and defense strategies that fuel escalation.
- Being flexible means going with the flow and not giving in. You can strengthen your position by first understanding the other party's perspective, then adapting to it, and in the third step reformulating the benefits for the other party to align with their needs.
- Don't just prepare your argument, but also prepare the other party for your argument.
- Consider all possible explanations for the other party's behavior and don't immediately assume incompetence or bad intentions.

- Ignore ultimatums: The more attention you give them, the more difficult it will be for the other side to give in when the situation changes.

VIRTUAL NEGOTIATION. BEST PRACTICE

Beware of the curse of knowledge, especially in virtual negotiations. Many negotiators feel confident in their areas of expertise and tend to intellectualize. This allows them to remain in their comfort zone. Unfortunately, as soon as online negotiators do this, they lose their sense of what it feels like for others not to know or to be driven by feelings. Also, in virtual negotiations, don't forget to emphasize what incentives and options can be created for all sides to make future negotiation attempts more successful. Even if time is short in a virtual negotiation, it's worth spending a few moments on this.

VIRTUAL NEGOTIATION. INTERVIEW

HERBERT THALER

Herbert Thaler has been working as a consultant and trainer in negotiation and sales management since 2017. He supports people in difficult negotiations to achieve their goals more quickly and easily.

J.P. Herbert, you worked as a sales manager for an international forestry and paper conglomerate, eventually leading the wood industry site in Austria as general manager. Conducting negotiations was day-to-day business for you, right?

H.T. That's right. As a decision maker, I was responsible for a negotiation volume of up to 150 million euros. During this time, I experienced some really hairy negotiations. I think back to the negotiations with the works council, where the basis for talks had to be completely rebuilt, or those with a major customer who wanted to win at all costs.

J.P. What is the biggest change for you when it comes to virtual negotiation?

H.T. The biggest change is that you get less information from your negotiating party. And information means power in negotiations.

J.P. Do you mean the power to withhold information?

H.T. No, it's less about what someone says and more about how (volume, emphasis, flow of speech) or what body language someone shows (facial expression, hand movement, posture). You can often only recognize approval and rejection, calmness, or tension through non-verbal communication.

J.P. How important is the virtual setting?

H.T. The first impression counts. Therefore, make sure that you show a large part of yourself and also some of your background. This means that your negotiating partner knows your setting, which builds trust. Artificial backgrounds may look professional, but they usually give the impression of simulating something that does not exist. Adjust the camera angle so that the camera captures you slightly from below. This makes you seem a little taller psychologically, giving you a touch of dominance.

J.P. What is your biggest challenge when it comes to virtual negotiation?

H.T. That would definitely be building a relationship quickly and keeping it stable when emotions rise. The virtual space entails a certain distance that needs to be overcome.

J.P. What advantage do you see in virtual negotiation?

H.T. Negotiators can very easily use prepared playbooks and other tools without the negotiating party seeing them.

J.P. You mean a negotiation playbook, a kind of manual for negotiation?

H.T. Yes, writing a negotiation playbook is my concrete tip for challenging virtual negotiations: Prepare thoroughly. Think the negotiation through to the end. What alternatives are possible, and what dead ends could arise? You can use these basic elements to build a negotiation playbook. Like a director's guide in a movie, such a playbook is a personal step-by-step guide so that you know exactly what you should do and say during negotiations.

J.P. How can virtual negotiators use the negotiation playbook?

H.T. You can put this playbook next to your negotiation documents. It gives you the confidence you need to do the right thing when the pressure or emotions are running high. Good luck!

VIRTUAL NEGOTIATION. QR

Here you can learn more about Herbert Thaler.

Tit for tat

Tit for tat is a well-known negotiating strategy made famous by the political scientist Robert Axelrod. Axelrod is considered the most prominent representative of rational choice theory and demonstrated the potential of the tit-for-tat strategy in a widely acclaimed computer experiment. The tit-for-tat strategy stems from game theory and shows negotiators in simple steps how to achieve the best possible result for both sides, even if the other side is behaving competitively. Tit for tat suggests the following procedure:

1. **Start with cooperation.**
   As the initiating person, you are sending an initial signal in the direction of cooperation. You are sending signals that show the other person that by being cooperative you are ready for a win-win.

2. **Remain flexible.**
   Whatever happens next, always behave in the same way as the other party did before. If negotiating parties go along with you and are also cooperative, then you will also remain cooperative. The stage is set.

3. **Switch to competitive behavior.**
   However, if your negotiating partner decides to adopt a competitive strategy, contrary to your first cooperative step, show them that you are also a master of this game and follow suit in the same way.

4. **Always remain clear, friendly, and conciliatory during the negotiation.**
   Show negotiating parties in a firm way that you are ready to return to cooperation at any point.
   The tit-for-tat strategy can be used in both virtual and face-to-face negotiations. Use the virtual breaks to retain a clear overview and discuss the next steps with your team based on the tit-for-tat strategy. Feedback from observers from your own ranks is also helpful in virtual negotiations.

In virtual negotiations, you can maintain a clear overview by starting to think trilaterally during the preparation phase. Don't forget that there are other people behind the virtual negotiating parties whose interests, needs, objections, and alternatives have an influence on those negotiating with you. Take into account the influence that third parties can have, even if you are defining the scope for negotiation.

VIRTUAL NEGOTIATION. TIP #23

Know your technology

Technology can also cause difficulties in virtual negotiations. Fortunately, there are helpful recommendations for familiarizing yourself step by step with technology in online meetings. In this way, you will gradually gain more composure as a virtual negotiator until it becomes second nature to negotiate remotely. No matter how experienced and tech-savvy most virtual negotiators are, they have all been let down by technology at some point. There are various ways to approach technology in virtual meetings:

1. Use the available online tutorials and instructions provided by the meeting software you are using.
2. Familiarize yourself with the functions of the meeting software by practicing with friends or colleagues and holding practice sessions.
3. Use the technology not only in virtual negotiations, but also regularly in your remote team meetings. You will then become more familiar with it and get used to its functions and processes.
4. Before the virtual negotiation, find out about possible problems that may arise during the meeting and how they can be resolved.
5. If difficulties arise, do not be afraid to ask for help. Help can come from various sources: colleagues who are already experienced can give you a helping hand. Technical support from the IT depart-

ment can be called in. You can search for solutions yourself in other sources such as online forums, social networks, or ChatGPT, a chatbot that works using artificial intelligence.

VIRTUAL NEGOTIATION. KNOWLEDGE

Chat GPT

To the question "How can Chat GPT support me in business negotiations?" the chatbot replied:

GPT-based chatbots like me can provide a number of ways to support you in business negotiations:

1. Automated responses: GPT-based chatbots can answer frequently asked questions automatically without the need for a human agent to intervene. This can save you time and ensure a faster response time.
2. Personalized interaction: A GPT-based chatbot can provide personalized answers based on customer data or information. This enables you to respond more effectively to your customers' needs and wishes in business negotiations.
3. 24/7 availability: A GPT-based chatbot can be available around the clock, which allows you to communicate with customers and close deals outside of normal business hours.
4. Language translation: A GPT-based chatbot can communicate in different languages, which can be helpful when dealing with customers in other countries or regions.
5. Documentation: GPT-based chatbots can keep a written record of the negotiation and save it. This way you can come back to specific points later or evaluate and review negotiations. Overall, GPT-based chatbots can be a useful complement to other forms of communication such as phone calls or face-to-face meetings in order to conduct business negotiations more effectively.

Typical technical disruptions that can occur during virtual negotiations are:

1. Connectivity problems
2. Poor audio and video quality
3. Compatibility problems
4. Disruptions due to background noise
5. Security problems

Connectivity problems

Problems with the Internet connection can lead to interruptions, delayed audio or video transmission or, in the worst case, to the termination of an online negotiation.

What you can do:

- Check that your Internet connection is stable and that sufficient bandwidth is available.
- Use a wired Internet connection for your virtual negotiation. This is often more stable than a connection via WIFI.
- Close any other programs that may impair the connection.
- Shut down devices that consume bandwidth if you do not need them.
- You can also improve the connection by deactivating audio and video functions when you are not actively speaking. This seems to contradict the recommendation to negotiate with the camera whenever possible. In this case, however, maintaining the connection has priority.
- Change your browser if you are having problems with your current browser.
- Connect from another device to check whether the problem is with your current device.
- Close the meeting and connect again to check whether the connection improves.
- Connect using a personal hotspot.
- Postpone the virtual negotiation if the problems cannot be resolved.

Poor audio and video quality

A delayed sound or a grainy image can impair communication in a virtual negotiation and make it difficult to understand the other negotiating party or follow what's being discussed during a negotiation.
What you can do:

- Check your equipment. Check whether your microphone, camera, and speakers are connected and set up correctly.
- Make sure that everything has been updated and that your programs are configured correctly.
- Check the position of your equipment. Make sure that the microphone and camera are at the ideal distance from you.
- Carry out a test run before the virtual negotiation and replace any equipment that may be deemed outdated or malfunctioning.
- Make sure that the surroundings are well lit so that the camera can capture you in the best light. Take into account the changing light conditions throughout the day.
- Use a headset to reduce background noise and ensure clear audio transmission.

Compatibility problems

Different devices or software versions may lead to certain functions not working or problems occurring during the setup of a meeting.
What you can do:

- Check whether your computer and software meet the minimum requirements for the planned meeting.
- Check whether you are using the latest version of the meeting software.
- Use a version of your operating system and browser that is officially recommended and supported by your meeting software.
- Install the latest drivers for your camera, microphone, and speakers so that everything works smoothly.

- Disable browser extensions that may affect compatibility.
- Perform regular updates of your meeting software.
- If you have problems with the meeting software, use the web app version and open your virtual negotiation directly in the browser.
- Dial into the conference by phone if you cannot solve compatibility problems in any other way to ensure that you can participate in the negotiation.

Disruptions due to background noise

Background noise is often louder for others than for the person making it. Microphone or camera problems can also distract virtual negotiators and make communication more difficult.

What you can do:

- Choose a quiet environment without background noise such as street noise, household noises, or conversations. Turn off the doorbell when working from your home office if you don't want the postman to ring twice.
- Use a headset with noise cancellation. Noise cancellation helps you to block out background noise and transmit your voice clearly.
- Use the mute function when you are not speaking and ask negotiating parties to do the same.
- Purchase a high-quality microphone or headset.
- Check the audio settings of your microphone and adjust its sensitivity.
- Close any windows and doors to reduce the noise from outside.
- Use noise reduction software to reduce background noise to a minimum.
- If necessary, let the other negotiating party know before the virtual negotiation that you are in a noisy environment and ask for their understanding.

Security problems

In the worst-case scenario unsecured connections or unprotected passwords can lead to unwanted participants entering the meeting or confidential information being inadvertently disclosed.

What you can do:

- Only use a reliable video conferencing platform that guarantees a secure connection.
- Use strong passwords to prevent unauthorized access.
- Send invitations to negotiating parties by email and avoid publicly accessible links to meetings.
- Limit access to your virtual negotiation by authenticating the participating negotiating parties or using the waiting room function.
- Activate the necessary security features such as screen locks, muting participants, disabling the recording function, and blocking the chat feature.
- Make your negotiating parties aware of the importance of security precautions such as data protection or confidentiality.
- Don't forget to regularly check the validity of security measures and update your systems and software to eliminate possible security gaps.
- Get support from IT security experts in your company and seek advice in advance.

VIRTUAL NEGOTIATION. BEST PRACTICE

Practice makes perfect! Can you still remember the first online meetings that were held during the lockdowns of the coronavirus pandemic? For many people, such a meeting was like rocket science. Widespread uncertainty could be observed. And then what happened? Together, people attempted to deal with the pitfalls of virtual technology. There was laughter and frustration, with lots of eye-rolling and plenty of doubts. Most of us had understanding for one another. Some caught on quickly, while others took a bit longer to develop a routine. And today? For most virtual negotiators, leading online meetings has become an integral part of their everyday work. Hybrid events are gradually becoming commonplace. It works particularly well when two large projectors hang side by side in a meeting room. Information is shared on one screen, while remote participants join in via camera on the second screen. Always remember: In an emergency, keep calm and carry on.

Miro, Mural, Conceptboard: Use collaborative tools to visualize key content

When the pandemic catapulted humanity into digitalization, collaborative tools sprang up like mushrooms. "Collaborative" means that all participants can work together and simultaneously on the same document in a shared virtual space. The content is therefore displayed in real time for all to see and released for collective editing. Today, such tools are regularly used in online meetings because they are useful for developing ideas for solutions. They can also be used to prioritize the various negotiation points. Working together on virtual whiteboards increases the attention span of the negotiators and enhances interaction.

The following questions arise in connection with their use in virtual negotiations:

- Why should collaborative tools be used in virtual negotiations?
- What are the most popular tools and how can negotiators use them professionally?
- What other kinds of special tools can be used that are still less well known?

Why should collaborative tools be used in virtual negotiations?

Using these tools can be very useful in many ways. They improve collaboration and help virtual negotiators to negotiate more efficiently and effectively. Sharing documents allows all negotiators to make decisions more quickly, eliminating the need to send documents back and forth. Communication is also supported. Negotiators can ask questions, give feedback, and solve problems more easily. The tools distract you from your emotions and draw your attention to the document you are currently working on. For this reason, this is also known as the "one-text procedure." With many tools available online and often for free, using them can reduce the cost of conducting negotiations.

What are the most popular tools and how can negotiators use them professionally?

Many of the collaborative tools are already well-known. They can be used for various tasks during negotiation. Here you will find a list of the most frequently used tools:

1. **Sharing presentations**: The screen sharing function is probably the best-known application used in virtual negotiations as well as online meetings.
2. **Joint document processing**: Tools such as Google Docs or Microsoft Teams are suitable for ensuring that everyone involved in the negotiation can work on a document at the same time and see changes in real time.
3. **Brainstorming**: For brainstorming, tools such as Trello, Miro, or Conceptboard can be used to collect, refine, and organize ideas. Negotiators can use them to maintain a clear overview of everything, even during complex negotiations, without creating a mess.
4. **Voting**: Negotiators can use tools such as Mentimeter or Google Forms to conduct votes and quickly obtain feedback on proposals from negotiating parties.

5. **Chatting**: All meeting software offers the opportunity to ask questions and exchange information during the negotiation. This is particularly helpful if the negotiating parties come from different cultures and use English as their negotiating language. There are negotiating parties who prefer to ask their questions in writing rather than orally. Popular text chat tools include Slack and the Microsoft Teams chat channel.
6. **Project management tools**: With project management software such as Asana or Trello, negotiators can organize and manage tasks and deadlines.

What other kinds of special tools can be used that are still less well known?

- **E-signature software**: This allows signatures to be affixed to digital documents, which no longer need to be printed out, signed, and re-scanned. In addition, signed documents can be forwarded immediately to the relevant departments. The best-known e-signature tool is DocuSign with a market share of 75 percent.

- **Digital data rooms**: Confidential data and documents can be securely managed and stored in digital data rooms. Digital data rooms are often used as part of due diligence processes during M&A, private equity, and venture capital transactions. The digital data room is an extranet that offers partners, buyers, and sellers the opportunity to access data that is normally stored in intranets. Popular tools include iDeals, CapLinked, DocSend, and Firmex.

- **Translation tools**: Use translation tools such as DeepL or Google Translate to translate texts into different languages in real time if the negotiation takes place with participants from different cultural backgrounds.

- **Online survey tools**: If you want to quickly gather feedback during a negotiation, you can use online survey tools such as Survey-Monkey, Mentimeter, Poll Everywhere, or slido.

VIRTUAL NEGOTIATION. TIP #25

Lighten the load: Make use of co-facilitation

As you are probably well aware, participating in virtual negotiations can be exhausting. But what is even more tiring is negotiating and facilitating the session at the same time. For this reason, team with a team member who will be your co-facilitator. A co-facilitator not only lightens your workload, but also helps all negotiators to achieve more successful negotiation results through clearer guidance and more structure.

Step 1: Determine the objective and method of the virtual negotiation with co-facilitators

The first questions when preparing for a virtual negotiation are always: Is our negotiation really necessary, or are there alternatives? You will call for virtual negotiations when you need the other party in order to solve problems (defining problems, researching causes, finding ideas, searching for solutions ...) or make decisions (evaluating and prioritizing alternatives, reaching consensus, agreeing on action steps). But remember: Mere socializing (getting to know each other, networking ...), information exchange (announcements, presentations of results, status reports ...), the coordination of projects, deadlines, and tasks or planning (determining and setting goals, developing strategies ...) are NOT negotiations.

Step 2: Clarify with co-facilitators where and how you would like to negotiate

Virtually, hybrid, on the phone, or face-to-face? If you are clear about the purpose and goal of the negotiation or sub-step of the negotiation, it is much easier to choose the appropriate communication method. Face-to-face negotiations are recommended when security and confidentiality are of great importance, relationships are to be strengthened (team building), sensitive issues are to be dealt with, and, of course, in the case of unresolved or open conflicts. Virtual negotiations are conducted when things need to be done quickly, time and money need to be saved, and/or negotiating parties are geographically distant from one another.

Step 3: Co-facilitators invite the right participants

Ask yourself the following questions: Who has the authority to make decisions? Whose support is indispensable? Who is affected by the measures to be adopted? Only invite participants who …

- have the relevant information and specialized knowledge to solve the problem.
- can make a decision.
- are affected by the decision or will implement it.

Tip: You can also invite part-time participants who are only present for certain items on the agenda.

Step 4: Prepare a clear agenda with co-facilitators

Depending on the complexity of the negotiation, you may have several items on the agenda to achieve sub-objectives. In the case of simple negotiations, your agenda will probably directly reflect the sub-objectives. Keep the following in mind when creating the agenda:

- Prioritize the items on the agenda.
- Tackle simple, easy-to-solve problems in the virtual negotiation first to give the participants a sense of achievement.
- Then deal with urgent and important matters.
- Afterwards, focus the negotiation on non-urgent but important matters.
- Each point is assigned a maximum duration.

In order to maintain the participants' concentration during long negotiations of more than an hour, you should also plan breaks. These provide time for regeneration and often significantly increase participants' effectiveness afterwards. The length of the breaks can depend on the difficulty of the topic and the duration of the negotiation. Analyze which agenda items are not relevant for all negotiators and plan in such a way that participants who are not interested in all items can either join later or leave the virtual negotiation earlier.

VIRTUAL NEGOTIATION. BEST PRACTICE

Allow time at the end of the negotiation for "parking lot" issues that came up during the negotiation. A parking lot is a secondary document on which open questions, issues to be resolved, or tasks arising from secondary topics are parked so that they do not get lost. The next step is to clarify who, what, and how to proceed with these points.

Step 5: Co-facilitators prepare participants in the most effective way possible

What the participants need before the negotiation is ...

- information about the purpose and objective of the virtual negotiation
- if applicable, the minutes from the last negotiation
- the list of participants and the agenda with contact persons for the individual agenda items
- information about necessary documents that participants should bring with them
- a prework sheet with links and information on topics that need to be prepared
- the invitation link for the meeting

Tip: In the invitation, co-facilitators can kindly point out to participants how important it is to prepare for the virtual negotiation so that they can work on the topics more efficiently. In the case of complex and multifaceted negotiation issues, it helps if co-facilitators send the negotiating party documents with the relevant information in advance by email. They should also be sure to label these documents precisely so that negotiators can easily navigate them during the video call and do not have to search for them first.

Tasks of the co-facilitator at the start of the negotiation

At the start of the negotiation, virtual negotiators expect clear signals as to who is holding the reins. The more clearly you signal from the outset that you are happy to take on the role of facilitator, the more likely it is that your control will be accepted and the easier it will be for you to be granted this role even at critical moments.

Task 1: Co-facilitators explain the purpose, goal, and agenda

Even if these points have already been mentioned in the invitation, it makes sense to point them out again specifically at the beginning of a virtual negotiation. In the next step, check whether the participants have the same understanding or agree with it. This means that negotiating parties now have the opportunity to get in touch if they are missing something. If a person feels that their personal goals are not covered by the agenda, they will not feel bound by the agenda. Therefore, add to the agenda if necessary, or decide to deal with missing points separately.

Task 2: Co-facilitators establish the ground rules for behavior and adhere to them

If you set ground rules at the beginning of a negotiation, you have the option of referring to them at any time during the course of the virtual negotiation if you feel that someone is not adhering to them. It is always difficult to introduce rules during an ongoing negotiation, as it only occurs to you when they are violated by one of the negotiators.

VIRTUAL NEGOTIATION. BEST PRACTICE

The more regularly the negotiators meet, the more familiar the ground rules are and the less time it takes when referring to them again.

VIRTUAL NEGOTIATION. KNOWLEDGE

Golden rules for virtual negotiations

- Punctuality: The virtual negotiation starts and ends on time, unless something else is decided during the meeting.
- Confidentiality: Matters discussed during the negotiation will be treated confidentially.
- Respect: All opinions are allowed; no one is criticized for their opinion.
- Regular breaks: Ten-minute breaks every 60 minutes.
- Only one person speaks at a time; there are no side conversations.
- Breaks: Each negotiator has the option to request a short break.

VIRTUAL NEGOTIATION. BEST PRACTICE

If a virtual negotiation does take longer, take a short break so that participants can reschedule their subsequent appointments.

Tasks of the co-facilitator during the negotiation

Task 1: Co-facilitators pay attention to the time

Participants are satisfied when the negotiation ends on time, happy when it goes faster, and annoyed when it ends too late.

VIRTUAL NEGOTIATION. KNOWLEDGE

Time management in virtual negotiations

- Even if it was already stated in the invitation, co-facilitators reiterate the planned duration of the virtual negotiation.
- Co-facilitators point out whether you are good on time or not.
- Co-facilitators are realistic when planning the agenda. In many cases, the agenda is so overloaded that it is impossible to even come close to covering the topics.
- Co-facilitators also play the role of "timekeeper," monitoring the timing of individual agenda items and the negotiation as a whole.

Task 2: Co-facilitators keep the right course

As the person steering the virtual negotiation, they have the task of ensuring that the negotiators do not deviate from the topic.

Task 3: Co-facilitators keep the negotiating team motivated

Negotiating is exhausting. The ability to concentrate varies from person to person, which is why it is also the task of co-facilitators to motivate the negotiating parties. Negotiating can also be fun!

Task 4: Co-facilitators foster a lively feedback culture in order to improve their negotiations

People often believe they know what others are thinking. Unfortunately, they are often wrong. It is better to take advantage of the many opportunities to get and give feedback during the negotiation. Through direct contact with the negotiating party, you'll show them through your behavior that you are aware of how they are feeling.

Task 5: Co-facilitators get everyone on board

Pay attention to changes in the mood of individual negotiating parties. Address any observations early on and confidently.

Task 6: Co-facilitators use working techniques professionally

As a co-facilitator, you are ideally an absolute methodological professional. You need the right tools: You need to know how to visualize content correctly, what rules a proper brainstorming session is based on, and how to manage discussions professionally.

Task 7: Co-facilitators visualize important points

Virtual negotiators are also primarily visual beings. Things that virtual negotiators also see are better remembered. Take every opportunity to record things in writing or in images. Collaborative tools provide you with creative options.

VIRTUAL NEGOTIATION. QR

Highly recommended! PresentationLoad's presentation templates make it easy to visualize content professionally. Scan the QR code to access the PresentationLoad website.

Why it pays to visualize content virtually

- Every virtual negotiator knows what is at stake. This is particularly important when returning to the topic after a short break in the conversation.
- Points are only discussed once and can then be ticked off.
- People only retain 20 percent of what they hear, 40 percent of what they see, and 60 percent of what they hear and see.
- All negotiators keep track of things when there are a lot of numbers involved.
- Co-facilitators have time to think while they write.
- At certain points, co-facilitators can help influence various phrasing.

Task 8: Co-facilitators keep the minutes

The most important skill of a note taker is the ability to listen and summarize without judging. Only key points are jotted down. The bullet points correspond verbatim to those of the negotiators and, if possible, are not reformulated. This underlines the value of the individual contributions. The documentation allows co-facilitators to refer to points that have already been discussed if the virtual negotiation starts to go around in circles.

Why brainstorming is an important creative technique in virtual negotiation

Developing ideas together is particularly important when negotiating according to the Harvard Concept. Here you will find the most useful recommendations for rule-compliant and constructive brainstorming. The goal of a brainstorming session is to produce as many ideas as possible on a topic. The biggest mistake that is repeatedly made in brainstorming is that the idea collection phase is not separated from the evaluation phase. This makes the process slow, strenuous, and not very productive. The basic rule is: first present the rules– among negotiation professionals, this does not have to be done in epic breadth–, then get started. This makes it easier for co-facilitators to refer to the rules later.

- Phase 1: Collect ideas and take notes.
- Phase 2: Evaluate the ideas and select which ones to pursue further.

VIRTUAL NEGOTIATION. KNOWLEDGE

The four most important rules of brainstorming

1. Every idea is valuable.
2. In phase 1, your task is solely to generate and collect ideas, without evaluating them.
3. Especially "crazy" ideas have great potential.
4. Let yourself be inspired by the ideas of your negotiating partners and refine them.

How discussions can be professionally steered by co-facilitators

Exchanging opinions is an important element of negotiation. The more heated the discussion, the more difficult it is for the co-facilitator to maintain control. This is why co-facilitators regularly summarize the intermediate results and follow up with "Did I understand you correctly ...?" They encourage quiet negotiating parties, address them by name, and ask them specifically for their opinion. Talkers and loudmouths are slowed down.

How co-facilitators can navigate any pitfalls and deal professionally with disruptions in virtual negotiations

Disruptions occur for various reasons. Sometimes some negotiators feel that their time is being wasted, or they feel that their needs are not being understood. Perhaps they also want to get their way at all costs because they know that the result will be watched very closely. As a negotiator, you can prevent many disruptions in advance by exercising great caution when inviting participants ("Who do I need, when, and why?"), practicing proactive time management, and choosing the optimal method. Recommendations on how to do so have already been discussed. However, if you are confronted with disruptions in your virtual negotiation, the following tips will help you to deal with them professionally: Refer to the ground rules established at the beginning. Give disruptive people one-on-one feedback, for example by calling them briefly during a break. In doing so, follow the usual guidelines for feedback. Describe exactly why you consider the person's behavior to be inappropriate/problematic and what effect it has had on you. If the behavior of an individual is very disruptive and you cannot take a break, address the issue directly in the meeting. You can use the PAST model for orientation.

The PAST model

The PAST model is used for quick de-escalation in a virtual negotiation. The acronym PAST stands for:

P = Perceiving the disturbance
A = Addressing/Acknowledging the disturbance
S = Suggesting a solution
T = Team approval

Perceiving the disturbance: Review your perception for objectivity. What do you see? What do you hear? Are there any patterns of the perceived behavior? What exactly is it that bothers you?

Addressing/Acknowledging: Address what you perceive to be hindering the constructive flow of the virtual negotiation: "I have noticed that …" Try a positive spin: "I can understand that …" This shows that you can understand where the cause of the problem lies.

Suggesting a solution: "That's why I suggest …" Ideally, you should combine the suggestion with an advantage for all negotiating parties: "The advantage for all of us is that …"

Team approval: "Do you agree with this?" If the other negotiators do not agree with your suggestion, they have the opportunity to correct it. However, if the negotiating parties agree and give their approval to the suggestion, then you have the official okay to continue with the negotiation.

How co-facilitators can conclude virtual negotiations professionally

With good planning, co-facilitators as captains of a negotiation can smoothly navigate digital cliffs and avoid virtual shoals. They can withstand all winds, with land in sight on the horizon and an approaching safe harbor. Now all that's left to do is to come in unharmed and drop anchor. Before you approve the minutes of the negotiation and, in most cases, the agreement, it is important to summarize the results once again and check whether all negotiating parties share the same understanding of the next steps.

- Responsibility for the individual tasks is specifically assigned to individuals and their agreement to assume responsibility is obtained.
- At the end, the decisions, next steps, and open questions are summarized.

Summaries of previously agreed decisions, further steps, and unresolved questions are an important tool for co-facilitators and participants in a virtual negotiation. The participants get the feeling that their views are taken into account and will remain committed. An objective summary of the facts shows the negotiating parties what conclusions are to be drawn or what measures are to be taken. An efficient summary highlights your competence as a negotiator.

Co-facilitators should conduct a final feedback session with their own team

It is beneficial for cooperation within your own negotiation team to obtain and give brief feedback after the virtual negotiation: How satisfied are we with the result? How satisfied are we with the cooperation between the negotiating parties? What did we do well? What can we do better next time? The closing feedback session can be held directly after the virtual negotiation, when impressions are still fresh, or in a separate team meeting.

Co-facilitators should distribute the minutes immediately

The easiest and most straightforward way is to use collaborative tools to create concurrent minutes during the negotiation. Resolution minutes are also often drawn up, which are usually based on the agenda items and can be supplemented.

The minutes of a virtual negotiation:

- are available to participants as soon as possible
- are written succinctly, concisely, and precisely
- clearly state who has to do what and by when
- contain formal elements:
  - ☐ date, time, and location of the meeting
  - ☐ participants
  - ☐ agenda items discussed, important arguments
  - ☐ decisions made, including information on what is to be done by whom and by when
  - ☐ date, time of any additional meeting

Co-facilitators keep track of the agreements

Virtual negotiation is of little use if you do not succeed in agreeing on concrete results whose actual implementation is monitored. A negotiation and the summary of the results will only be taken seriously if the measures are adhered to. For larger tasks, schedule additional intermediate appointments to review implementation. Show interest in the results and offer support with questions instead of acting as the controller. Beware of re-delegation! As a reminder, co-facilitators can send friendly emails to delayed movers.

Chapter 7 concludes this book. You have been given four final tips on how to stay on top of things in virtual negotiations. Now you have the opportunity to create a personal checklist so that you always have the eight most important points at a glance and readily available.

1. ....
....
2. ....
....
3. ....
....
4. ....
....
5. ....
....
6. ....
....
7. ....
....
8. ....
....

Conclusion – Virtual negotiation isn't worse. It's different.

Virtual negotiation will only gain in importance in the coming years. The shift of many companies' business activities into the digital space, along with the associated proliferation of online tools, is by now a mostly smooth process that is continuously being optimized through increasingly sophisticated software, more powerful hardware, and more stable networks. Negotiators are becoming more experienced in using the tools. In this way, virtual negotiation will gradually become a natural complement to face-to-face negotiation. Depending on the industry and topic, it may replace face-to-face negotiations entirely. It is more flexible and convenient. Negotiators can participate from anywhere in the world without having to travel, saving both time and money. The virtual negotiations can be easily recorded, which can later serve as evidence or a source of information. Advances in the field of artificial intelligence will revolutionize negotiation to an as yet unknown extent. It's an exciting time.

And yet we are human beings with emotions. We're not machines. We interpret other people's statements, which can lead to misunderstandings and incorrect assumptions. But we can also reassure, soothe, and persuade others. In the long run, completely giving up communication is not possible. Virtual negotiators need to make sure their personal resources are fit for the new game with the new rules. Yoga, for example, is very well suited to this. The experienced yoga teacher Alexander Eichhorn imparts a deeper understanding of the holistic yoga philosophy in office yoga sessions. He uses small, uncomplicated practical exercises to show how these insights can easily be incorporated in everyday working life. Yoga exercises immediately encourage a lot in us: body awareness, coordination, balance, flexibility, concentration, balance, imagination, and creativity. That makes them an excellent resource for successfully negotiating virtually in the long term. Good luck!

ALEXANDER EICHHORN

Alexander Eichhorn traveled as far as China back in the 1990s, where he competed as a member of the German national team for WuShu (Chinese for martial arts). He completed his yoga teacher training in New York. For over 16 years, he has been practicing as a professional yoga teacher in Munich, and since 2020, he has been successfully offering virtual business yoga sessions. 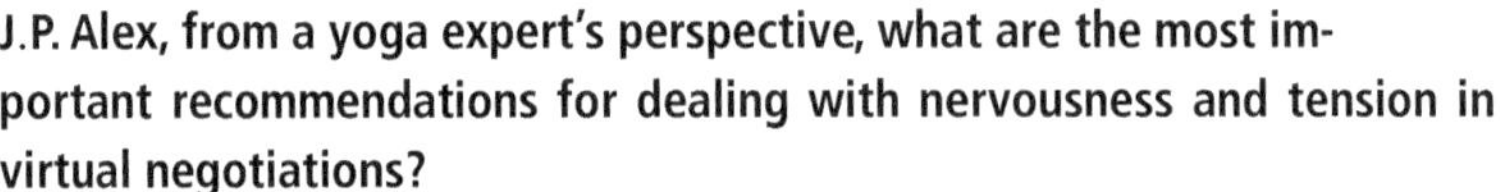

J.P. Alex, from a yoga expert's perspective, what are the most important recommendations for dealing with nervousness and tension in virtual negotiations?

A.E. 1. Mindfulness with yourself: first of all to become aware of the fact that nervousness and tension exist and then to recognize what beliefs and triggers activate them. In this way, these can be changed over time, and greater resilience can develop.

2. Practice not getting lost in thought spirals. This can be done well by practicing conscious breathing and body scanning.

3. Conscious, deep, and even breathing: Always take a few minutes to breathe consciously, especially before negotiations. For example, inhale for four seconds, hold your breath for four seconds, exhale for four seconds, hold for four seconds, and repeat this for five to ten rounds or three to five minutes.

4. Body scanning: Simply bring your attention to your body and practice consciously relaxing it. Breathe deeply and evenly and scan through your body one area at a time, trying to relax/release tension.

5. Don't take everything too seriously: Realize that small mistakes happen and that this is human.

With 4 & 5, you can become more and more able to relax and be present within yourself.

J.P. What can virtual negotiators do if they lose focus during a negotiation?

A.E. If I misspeak, lose focus, or something similar, I deal with it as casually, naturally, and confidently as possible – it's only human. If the person I'm speaking to notices that I'm relaxed and at peace with my "shortcomings," it often comes across as very likeable and also lightens the mood.

J.P. Can yoga routines help virtual negotiators to stay focused over a longer period of time?

A.E. Yoga exercises can help us become more relaxed, calmer, more present, clearer, more vital, and more focused in the face of the demands of the working world. Tension and stress can eat up a lot of energy. If we keep these in check by exercising regularly, we have more energy and focus to complete our tasks more efficiently and easily. If I am at peace within myself and have enough energy at my disposal, I automatically have easier and better access to my potential – to my abilities, my creativity, etc. A regular routine that is adapted to the individual can help a lot with this. To achieve optimum results, you don't have to practice a lot or for a long time, but rather regularly and with the right inner attitude.

VIRTUAL NEGOTIATION. QR

Here you can learn more about Alexander Eichhorn.

THANKS

Muito obrigada!
I would like to thank Doreen, Agnes and Lisa, my muses M&C, and my sons Jannic, Julien, and Justin.

Lisbon, January 2024

APPENDIX

About the Author

Jutta Portner lives at Lake Starnberg and is Managing Director of C-TO-BE. THE COACHING COMPANY. For over twenty years, she has worked as a business coach and management trainer, primarily for companies in the automotive and chemical industries, as well as for banks and aerospace companies. As a negotiation consultant and ghost negotiator, she advises managing directors before and during challenging negotiations. Since 2011, she has supported the International Management Program of the German Ministry of Economics as a negotiation trainer, having gained intercultural experience with participants from 21 nations. As a keynote speaker, she engages audiences at customer and supplier workshops. Her great passion is writing, which always revolves around the topic of NEGOTIATION.

A Word from the Author

Do you have a difficult negotiation ahead of you? Are you in the middle of a deadlock? Is your next salary negotiation coming up? Do you repeatedly find yourself at dead ends and don't know how to get out of them? Would you like feedback on your personal negotiating skills? Or would you like to prepare your employees for upcoming virtual negotiations?

Then C-TO-BE. THE COACHING COMPANY is right where you belong. Feel free to contact us. We would be happy to help you and look forward to your inquiry!

Jutta Portner

Contact

C-TO-BE. THE COACHING COMPANY
Jutta Portner (contact person for content)
Agnes Kosmalski/Nina Trajanovska (organization and coordination)
Seeuferstraße 59, D-82541 Münsing, Germany
Cell phone: +49 -172 83 16 701, welcome@c-to-be.de, www.c-to-be.de

Endnotes

1   https://www.c4-quadriga.eu/c4-negotiation-survey/ (30.01.2024).

2   https://pactum-advisory.de/13-tipps-um-erfolgreich-online-zu-verhandeln/#Wir_sind_gestresst (30.01.2024).

3   Reed, Stanley Foster, and Alexandra Reed Lajoux: The Art of M&A: A Merger Acquisition Buyout Guide. New York City, McGraw-Hill, 1999. Pg. 486.

4   Bulow, Jeremy, and Paul Klemperer: "Auctions versus Negotiations." American Economic Review No. 86, 1996, Pg.180.

5   Subramanian, Guhan: Negotiauctions. So gewinnen Sie mit neuen Verhandlungsstrategien. Campus Verlag, Frankfurt am Main, 2012, Chapter 3, Eine wichtige Entscheidung: Auktion oder Einzelverhandlung, Pg. 60 (translated by B.A).

6   Portner, Jutta: Flexibel verhandeln. Die vier Fälle der NEGO-Strategie. GABAL Verlag, Offenbach, 2017. Chapter 2.2 Sie wollen führen? Folgen Sie dem Prozess, Pg. 65ff.

7   Portner, Jutta: Besser verhandeln. Das Trainingsbuch. GABAL Verlag, Offenbach, 2015. Pg. 92.

8   https://hbr.org/2014/08/what-people-are-really-doing-when-theyre-on-a-conference-call (30.01.2024).

9   https://www.ibe-ludwigshafen.de/zoom_fatigue/ (30.01.2024).

10   Kennedy, Gavin, Everything is Negotiable, Random House Business, 2008.

11   Gavin Kennedy, Negotiation, Edinburgh Business School/Heriot-Watt University, Module 4, Debate in Negotiation.

12   https://cdn2.hubspot.net/hubfs/4000014/Data%20Capture%20Documents/Global%20Negotiation%20Research.pdf?__hstc=235931038.f116d2a4ceddd8ced4554f44c91fe cb5.1680421741217.1680421741217.1680421741217.1&__hssc= 235931038.3.1680421741217&__hsfp=2459201453&hsCtaTracking=580af107-32b7-4362-aa21-3bb881c2295c%7C1591987a-80ca-4f77-94b0-39a8197db28b (30.01.2024)

13   https://listeninginstitute.com/richard-mullender/ (30.01.2024).

14   https://hbr.org/2022/07/working-through-your-on-camera-meeting-anxiety (30.01.2024)

15   Portner, Jutta: Besser verhandeln. Das Trainingsbuch. GABAL Verlag, Offenbach, 2015. Pg. 326ff.

[16] https://www.4tiitoo.com/nuia-full-focus-for-eye-contact-in-video-calls (30.01.2024).

[17] Loschky, Eva: Gut klingen – gut ankommen: Effektives Stimmtraining mit der Loschky-Methode®. Munich, Goldmann Verlag, 2009.

[18] Voss, Chris with Tahl Raz, Never Split the Difference: Negotiating As If Your Life Depended On It? London, Random House Business, 2017.

[19] https://en.wikipedia.org/wiki/Game_theory (30.01.2024).

[20] Kennedy, Gavin, Everything is Negotiable, Random House Business, 2008.

[21] Kennedy, Gavin: Negotiation, Module 9, Edinburgh Business School/ Heriot-Watt University, Edinburgh, 2002.

[22] Inspired by Karrass, Chester L.: In Business As In Life – You Don't Get What You Deserve, You Get What You Negotiate. Beverly Hills (USA), Stanford Street Press, 1996. Pg. 203ff.

[23] Koch, Dirk: »Die Brüsseler Republik«. DER SPIEGEL 52/1999, Pg. 136 (translated by B.A.).

[24] Voss, Chris with Tahl Raz, Never Split the Difference: Negotiating As If Your Life Depended On It? London, Random House Business, 2017.

[25] Ury, William: Getting Past No. Negotiating in Difficult Situations. New York, Bantam Dell Publishing, 1991.

[26] Fisher, Roger/Ury, William/Patton, Bruce Das Harvard-Konzept. Die unschlagbare Methode für beste Verhandlungsergebnisse, Campus Verlag, 2015, Pg. 79 (translated by B.A.).

[27] Malhotra, Deepak and Max. H Bazerman: Negotiation Genius: How to Overcome Obstacles and Achieve Brilliant Results at the Bargaining Table and Beyond. New York City, Harvard Business School, Bantam Books, 2007.

[28] Malhotra, Deepak: Negotiating the Impossible: How to Break Deadlocks and Resolve Ugly Conflicts (Without Money or Muscle). Oakland, Berrett-Koehler Publishers, 2016.

Image credits

All icons and illustrations used in the book are courtesy of Presentationload (https://www.presentationload.de).
Author photos: Alexander Eichhorn; Bettina Kappe; Jörg Rottenburger; Wolfgang Schatz; Miriam Steimer; Herbert Thaler: private
Jutta Portner: @ Lars Ternes.

Index

Bibliography

Axelrod, Robert: *Die Evolution der Kooperation*. Translated and with an epilogue by Werner Raub and Thomas Voss. De Gruyter Oldenbourg, Potsdam, 2009.

Brandenburger, Adam M. und Nalebuff, Barry J.: *Co-Opetition*. Profile Books, London ,1997.

Cialdini, Robert B.: *Influence, New and Expanded: The Psychology of Persuasion*. HarperCollins, New York, 2021.

Fisher, Roger and Shapiro, Daniel: *Beyond Reason: Using Emotions as You Negotiate*. Random House, New York, 2006.

Fisher, Roger, Ury, William and Patton, Bruce: *Getting to Yes: Negotiating an agreement without giving in*. Random House, New York, 2021.

Huthwaite International Institute: "How well are you negotiating?" United Kingdom, study from 2014.

Gigerenzer, Gerd: *The Intelligence of Intuition*. Cambridge University Press, Cambridge, 2023.

Karrass, Chester L.: *Give and Take: The Complete Guide to Negotiating Strategies and Tactics*. Ty Crowell Co, New York, 1974.

Karrass, Chester L.: *The Negotiating Game*. HarperBusiness, New York, 1994.

Karrass, Chester L.: *In Business As In Life – You Don't Get What You Deserve, You Get What You Negotiate*. Stanford Street Press, Beverly Hills, 1996.

Kennedy, Gavin: *Essential Negotiation. An A-Z Guide*. Profile Books Ltd., London, 2004.

Kennedy, Gavin: *Everything is NEGOTIABLE – How to get the Best Deal Everytime*. Random House Business, London, 2008.

Kennedy, Gavin: *Negotiation*. Edinburgh Business School/Heriot-Watt University, Edinburgh, 2011.

Lax, David A. and Sebenius, James K.: *3-D Negotiation. Powerful Tools to Change the Game in Your Most Important Deals*. Harvard Business Review Press, Boston, 2006.

Levine, Robert: *The Power of Persuasion*. Wiley, New York, 2007.

Malhotra, Deepak and Bazerman, Max H.: *Negotiation Genius: How to Overcome Obstacles and Achieve Brilliant Results at the Bargaining Table and Beyond*. Harvard Business School, Bantam, New York, 2007.

Malhotra, Deepak: *Negotiating the Impossible. How to Break Deadlocks and Resolve Ugly Conflicts (Without Money or Muscle)*. Berrett-Koehler Publishers, Oakland, 2016.

Mastenbroek, Willem F. G.: *Verhandeln: Strategie – Taktik – Technik*. Dr. Th. Gabler Verlag, Wiesbaden, 1992.

Molcho, Samy: *Körpersprache des Erfolgs*. Ariston, Munich, 2005.

Navarro, Joe: *What every Body is saying*. ⊠ William Morrow Paperbacks, New York, 2008.

Navarro, Joe: *Louder than words*. William Morrow, reprint edition, New York, 2011.

Portner, Jutta: *Besser verhandeln. Das Trainingsbuch*. GABAL Verlag, Offenbach, 2010.

Portner, Jutta: *Flexibel verhandeln. Die vier Fälle der NEGO-Strategie*. GABAL Verlag, Offenbach, 2017.

Rackham, Neil and Carlisle, John: "The Effective Negotiator – Part 1: The Behaviour of Successful Negotiators." *Journal of European Industrial Training*, Vol. 2, No. 6, 1978.

Storch, Maja and Krause, Frank: *Selbstmanagement – ressourcenorientiert. Theoretische Grundlagen und Trainingsmanual für die Arbeit mit dem Zürcher Ressourcen Modell (ZRM)*. Expanded and completely revised edition. Verlag Hans Huber, Bern, 2014.

Subramanian, Guhan: *Negotiauctions: New Dealmaking Strategies for a Competitive Marketplace*. W W Norton & Co., New York, 2010.

Ury, William: *Getting Past No. Negotiating Your Way from Confrontation to Cooperation*, Bantam Books, New York, 1991.

Ury, William: *The Power of a Positive No. How to Say No and Still Get to Yes*. Bantam Books, New York, 2007.